The Colossal Life of Mr. Average

by

Bob Ferguson

Copyright © 2015 by Bob Ferguson

All rights reserved. No part of this book, except for educational purposes, may be reproduced or transmitted in any form or by any means whatsoever.

ISBN 10: 1517416094
ISBN 13: 978-1517416096

Publisher: Chicken Publications
Printed in the USA
Published October 2016
Second Edition

DEDICATION

To those who read this and say "I'm going to write my own book."

CONTENTS

Acknowledgements

1 Camp Easter Seal

2 Business Stories

3 Family Tales

4 Old Yarns

5 Non-Creative Fiction

6 Don't Hold Back

7 I'm In!

8 Bar Stool Chats…

9 Pickleball Addiction

10 Meanderings and…

Bob Ferguson

This book is meant to be dog eared, covered with coffee and notes in the margins for writing your stories. Have fun with it!

ACKNOWLEDGMENTS

To the many characters who have waltzed across my life's stage, thank you for the dance. My wife of 50 years, Ardis has played the title role and the kids, Robb, Ryan, Rachel, and Randall have contributed mightily to the drama in our lives.

CHAPTER 1

Fun at Camp Easter Seal

Like a bronco busting out of the chute, I bucked, hurdled, and bounded down the stairs of the Oakland Naval Hospital. It was the proverbial "First day of the rest of my life." School was finished. I had survived Vietnam. The Marine Corps had just informed me that Captain Robert E. Ferguson was being launched back into civilian life. The prospect of finally being able to live life on my terms made me ecstatic. "The world was my oyster." It would be opened. I would delight in its offerings. Life would be fun again.

My teen years spent as a counselor at Camp Easter Seal stamped me so indelibly that all I ever wanted to be was the Camp Director. No other jobs would be considered. Ardi knew I had coveted this job since I was fifteen years old. An entire decade had passed. The stakes were higher than any poker game, but I was all in. I was compelled to apply.

Mr. Torson was still the Executive Director of the Oregon Easter Seal Society. With a fountain pen, in my best handwriting, I composed the following letter.

Dear Mr. Torson,

As I prepare to leave the Marine Corps my thoughts return to Camp Easter Seal so I am writing to inquire about the position of Camp Director. You may be assured that my physical injuries incurred in Vietnam are minor and will not interfere with the job requirements.

If the position is open at this time, please consider this letter as an application for Camp Director of Camp Easter Seal.

Mr. Torson, even when I was a young counselor at the camp, I knew I wanted to pursue the job of Camp Director. My desires remain unchanged.

Sincerely,

Bob Ferguson

Captain, USMC

Within a few days Mr. Torson called and told me that the position was open "But," he said "I'm not sure we can afford a Marine Corps Captain. The job pays about the same as a teacher, it's all year, but you do get a four week vacation."

Butterflies attacked my stomach. This grand news made me weak in the knees. I had arranged a two week leave and we planned a trip to Seattle to see Ardi's parents. We would be driving through Portland in the early evening so we arranged to meet Mr. Torson at the Easter Seal office just off of Barbur Boulevard. "Mush," as I now called him, offered me $10,000 per year with no benefits. It was $6,000 less than I had been earning. Not to mention the healthy military bennies.

"When can I start?" I said.

"Mush" was the antithesis of a micromanager. All of the directors he hired said the same thing "He told you that you were the camp director and then let you direct the camp." Our only requirement was a daily report. It listed the number of kids and staff in camp along with the daily activities like morning fishing, afternoon swimming, and evening campfires. The report was for insurance purposes and a federal food program for non-profits. The food program gave us loads of beans, rice, lentils, and marvelous amounts of cheese.

Camp was all fun and games when I had been a counselor. Flirting with the volunteer kitchen-aids was a mainstay of camp life. As the director, the care, feeding, and safety of several hundred people for an entire summer was a huge responsibility. I relished the challenge!

All camps are about nature. But Camp Easter Seal had the intrinsic charm of being only accessible by a fifteen minute boat ride on a pristine lake where the vegetation grew over the water's edge. It was much like in the days when the Coos Indians paddled their canoes to hunt ducks and frogs in the shallows. The other side of that idyllic coin was the demanding logistics of moving campers, staff, and supplies in boats. It was WORK!

The camp program was divided into five sessions of about eighty people each. Every session lasted ten days. Campers, without regard to disabilities whether it was a physical or mental handicap, were grouped by ages. The first session had campers as young as six years old, then the pre-teens, followed by the raucous teenagers, next were the young adults, and camp concluded in late August with an adult session.

The camp newspaper was "Totem Times." One of the first thing arrivals saw was the 30 foot totem pole carved by Byron Kroge, the director of Children's Hospital School in Eugene, Oregon. He was a superb wood carver and the pole looked like a real Indian totem pole, complete with the wings of a Thunderbird. The campers chose the name for the paper, wrote the articles, and it was a great way for parents to get a glimpse of camp life. It was a delight to read what the campers wrote about the activities.

It has been forty two years since I last looked at my camp scrapbook. It was made by Peg, our Arts and Crafts counselor during the summer of '72. Sandwiched in-between two, 13" x 19" plywood covers adorned with paintings representing camp life are craft projects and articles written by our campers and staff for the camp newspaper. The next few pages are their words, sparingly edited with only a few notations for clarity.

Totem Times

New Things At Camp "We have two new ponies that pull a cart and a tall riding horse. We have bunnies and the mother is going to have babies." By Janet Fraser.

The First Campfire "The first night at camp we had a campfire. It was very funny. The knock, knock jokes were also funny. I also liked the costumes very much. I think the spit around the world was funny when it got some kids wet. The song I liked best was "If You're Happy and You Know It" (clap your hands, stomp your feet, and shout Amen! I highly recommend you put down this book and sing it, teach it your grand kids and you'll be a hit!) by Kirby Alcott.

Flag Raising "Each day the cabin with the cleanest room is responsible for raising and lowering the flag. The first day of the session the winning cabin was Dog House One. The campers are Troy Vaughan, Mike Adams and Fred Franco." By Jim Sells.

Horseback Riding Jim Marcoe has a cart pulled by two ponies, Hi-Ho and Silver. Dee Dee helps with the horseback riding. She taught us to sit up straight and hold the reins with both hands. The horses are named Prince and Trixie.

Camp Time Favorites Tony Skinner – Fishing, Brenda Greenwalt – Horseback riding, Karen Cabe – Swimming, Stephanie Garey – Riding in the horse cart, Scott Wolfe – Campfire singing, Sam Willoughby – boating, Jennifer Roberts – Watching counselors jump in the lake!

Note: *During the younger sessions camp favorites were fishing, boating, crafts, B-B guns, horseback riding, and campfires. The favorites of the Teen and Adult sessions revolved around social activities as told in Volume 4 of the <u>Totem Times.</u>*

<u>Coketails Anyone</u>? The Coketail Party really turned out cool! My date was right on time and he gave me a very lovely corsage. The dance floor was full at all times and the tables were out of sight! Since it was getting kind of hot in there with all the dancing and stuff, I noticed that a few couples went out under the stars. The live music was really great! At 10:15 our dates walked us to our tents. By Laurie Jones.

<u>Editor's Note</u> "The new staff members have been great. They have brought with them fresh, new ideas which have really enriched the camping experience. One popular addition was that of having voluntary group discussions. Topics included Dating, Marriage, and Sex with respect to the physically handicapped. Fourth session this year proved to be most rewarding. Thank you staff, volunteers, and campers. By Jerry Pattee, <u>Totem Times</u> Editor.

The first day of camp immersed the campers in the magnificence of the lake, quite often spying the resident Osprey on the way to camp. They arrived at the dock at the south end of Ten Mile Lake, south of Reedsport, Oregon. To avoid a crush at the dock, their arrival times were staggered on their acceptance forms. Counselors at the camp would entertain the early arrivals with fun and games while the others loaded kids, wheelchairs, crutches, and luggage into the boats. For most parents, this was a ten day reprieve from the overwhelming responsibility of the 24/7 care of their disabled child. It was an indirect benefit of the camp.

The young kids in the first session were a lot of physical work, but fun. One of their main activities was fishing. The dock on our boathouse was perfect for catching perch and an occasional catfish. The lake teemed with the trash fish and every child caught lots of fish. We buried them as fertilizer for the camp flowers. The afternoon was often spent swimming in our own roped off area of the lake. Sand was hauled in over a back road to make a nice sized, beach. A 10' X 20' floating dock was the outer boundary of the area and ropes with floats attached made a large rectangular swimming area about 50' X 50' with a gentle slope into the lake.

A typical day would start at 7:30 with dressing the campers, breakfast at 8:00 AM, then the morning would be filled with fishing, arts and crafts, horse or buggy rides, petting zoo, boat rides, BB gun target shooting, nature hikes, and nearly every night we had a campfire with skits and singing.

Singing was a gigantic part of camp life. There were songs at every meal, flag raising, on the dock while waiting for fish to bite, and campfires. The campfires had a certain rhythm. They started off with a rousing rendition of "If you're happy and you know it, clap your hands," then a funny skit, followed by "This Land is Your Land," and ended with gentle songs like "Kumbaya My Lord." Every session, counselors and campers would get a song stuck in their head and would be heard singing, whistling, or humming the tunes all day long. It was infectious and contagious. Music made camp a happy place to be.

The male volunteer counselors were always too cool to sing. I made it mandatory. A lot of campers could only mumble the songs through paralyzed mouths, but would be singing at least the chorus. Able bodied staff were required to set the example that "everybody sings." The staff would check in the day before campers arrived. We had a staff planning session that included reviewing each camper's handicapping condition. It was a huge education for young counselors. Our song leader would then lead us in a few songs to set the tone that every person was required to sing.

The personal growth of the counselors during the summer was enormously satisfying. Our young, 16 yr. old counselors were relied upon to run our boats filled with campers. I never worried about them. At the campfires the "ham" in them came out. When required to lead a song during our training sessions a few discovered they were excellent song leaders.

One of my favorite skits was a spoof about "The Ugliest Man In The World." It went like this; two accomplices were in the audience when the Ugliest Man was led into the campfire circle covered by a blanket. The campers were warned that the mere sight of such ugliness caused certain death. The accomplices would peek under the blanket, give a ghastly scream, and fall down dead. Then an unsuspecting camper would peek under the blanket, "lo and behold," the Ugliest Man in The World would fall down dead! I never got tired of it. The more grotesque the death throes, the more the kids loved it. "Chewing the scenery" was noisily rewarded.

During the teen sessions, dances became more popular than campfires. Singing "Swing Low Sweet Chariot" didn't hold a candle to a live, garage band pounding out "Proud Mary" by Creedence Clearwater. Socialization was far more important than the traditional camp activities. Nature hikes gave way to "Rap Sessions." These were no holds barred discussions and ventured into topics that all adults and older teens like to talk about. That was, of course, sex. One of our goals was to help campers be as independent, socially adept, and as self-actualized as possible.

During the Adult Sessions we had "Baby Care" as an activity. The girls loved giving our six month old child, Robb, a bath and doting on him. Three years later, when Ryan was brought to camp at only a week old the campers loved helping to give him a bath, hold him and all of the stuff they would never be able to do in their own lives. We took surveys after each camp session. "Baby Care" was invariably marked as the girl's favorite activity.

When I reported these activities in the daily report eyebrows were raised back at the Easter Seal office. The question was asked "Are 'Dancing' and 'Baby Care' really camping activities?" My answer was "If the campers like it and it helps them socially, what difference does it make?" It was an argument I had to make many times. The surveys proved we were on the right track. I told other camp directors. They began having dances at their camps which became the highlight of their camping programs. The kids in wheelchairs rocked themselves or got help from their partner. The deaf kids could feel the beat through the floor of the dining hall. Everyone created their own unique, dance style. It was marvelous to watch and the staff enjoyed it as much as the campers.

Every year we tried to top ourselves in activities. We strained to create the "Perfect Summer." Live bands replaced records. The 6:00 AM boat rides were a hit with the nature lovers, the staff water show included pulling a few campers on gigantic inner tubes behind our speedboats, and a long Slip 'N Slide at the swimming hole was a hit with the little kids. One Fourth of July we took all the kids to the fireworks display at the south end of the lake. We led a patriotic tribute of singing for everyone in the park. We only did it one year, there were too many inebriated boaters to contend with on the trip back to camp. But the all-time activity was taking the entire camp of over ninety people on an overnight camp out at Sunset Bay State Park, near Coos Bay, Oregon.

The logistics were daunting. The price tag alone for ninety people would have to be mitigated. A call to the director of Oregon State Parks was made. At first he was difficult to deal with. When I pointed out that we had many campers from Fairview Training Center, a state owned facility and they all came to camp free of charge, he changed his tune. He quickly got on board with accommodating us.

We borrowed buses from local churches, cooked over an open fire and took a chance on the coastal weather. It was the first real beach trip for almost all of our campers. In four years I had never called the Easter Seal office to get permission for any activity. Why start now? My philosophy was "Act now and pray for forgiveness later."

Squeals of delight came from kids feeling the tug of a kite string wrapped around hands that couldn't hold a spool. Smiles beamed from the faces of campers holding a snail gently lifted from a tidal pool. The wheel chairs and crutches took a salt-water beating as campers waded where the waves kissed the sand turning it into a deep buckskin color as they washed up onto a near level beach. Sand castle building piqued creative minds, but covered campers with a layer of pesky grit. But this was a once in a lifetime event for nearly all of the campers. A little sand would not be a deterrent to a Colossal experience.

Sunset Bay State Park was well equipped with first-class restrooms and showers that were better than the camp's. We set up an operation similar to a car-wash. We ran campers and gear through the cold, outside rinsing station. This was followed by the warm, inside shower. The "B-r-r-r's were followed by A-h-h-h's."

That afternoon, on the way back to camp we passed a Dairy Queen that was running a special on five-cent ice cream cones. I'll never forget the look on the clerk's face when I said "I'd like 95, nickel, ice cream cones please." The cones were a hit!

The beach trip, while a great idea, was a back breaking job for our staff. We only did it once. But the campers and staff remembered it as one of the best-ever activities. You never know if you have reached your limit until you smack up against it, and that trip was ours. But that's a good thing. One of my biggest regrets in my life has been that I haven't done enough testing of the limits. "Nothing ventured, nothing gained."

My last year at the camp was difficult and it wasn't the kids or counselors. We knew we were making a difference in the lives of our campers. "Thank You" cards poured into the office, but I decided to make a change that became a lightning rod for criticism.

The single most important characteristic that separated campers was not age, it was the type of disability. If a camper was mentally challenged, the types of songs and games had to be adapted to their mental functioning level. On the other hand, they were the most physically active on nature hikes, the swimming area, and all things physical. Those with physical disabilities enjoyed the skits, talent shows, card games, and all things intellectual. Our programming operated at the lowest common denominator for all campers. It wasted the abilities of campers and the creativity of our staff.

To enhance the experience for all campers, I created what we called a "Special Focus" session for the mentally handicapped. (I have no idea what the current politically correct term is for this condition. My intent is to enlighten, not to offend.) It would now allow for optimal programming in each session. The mentally challenged no longer had to wait for the slowest wheelchair. The physically handicapped could engage in a broader array of social and intellectual activities. It was such a workable solution, created from our personal experience, that I fully expected this idea to sweep the nation. It didn't.

Camper assignments had been made for the summer of 1972. The "fat was in the fire," but seemingly overnight the national mood changed to "Mainstreaming" people with mental difficulties. Advisors from the National Easter Seal Society came all the way from Chicago to "confer" with me. Other big wigs in the camping world phoned and told me I was out of step with what was best for our campers. I wavered a bit.

Mush, true to his nature, said "It's your camp to run the way you think is best." We ran the "Special Focus" session. It was the easiest on the staff because most campers were self-reliant. The planning was simplified, and the physical activities were expanded. During the "Adult" physically handicapped session, the "Campers Council" blossomed and they planned many of their own activities. It was an overwhelming success. It was a win-win situation, but criticism still poured in from all directions. I wouldn't budge.

That year my brother, Danny was the assistant camp director. No nepotism here, he had a degree in Recreation, had been a teen counselor at the camp for many years, had boundless energy, and immensely influenced our new direction. The adult activities had a much higher social appeal to the physically handicapped campers. The "Rap Sessions were extremely popular and Camper's Council members joined our staff meetings to plan several of their own activities. The campers also took over publication of the *Totem Times*. For some, Camper's Council or writing for the newspaper was their primary activity. Their abilities were maximized, but the voices of reproach for "segregating the mentally handicapped" grew louder. Mush encouraged me with his favorite quote *"Behold the Turtle, He Makes Progress only when he sticks his neck out."* To this day, I still think the world is out of step.

Tragedy struck two days before camp officially ended for the summer of 1972. A Vietnam veteran who had returned to "The World" picked up where he had left off, drinking beer with his high school friends. He had survived the diseases of the jungle and the bullets of the Viet Cong. He reverted to his old habits and haunts. The small bridge leading into Florence, Oregon crossed a narrow stream. The old cement structure was designed for form and function. The decorative, four foot high cement barrier was capped with a two foot wide railing. He had walked across it many times. The beer made him bullet proof. He fell thirty feet.

John Metcalf sustained a brain injury that affected his entire left side, slurred his speech and left a large dent in his head. He came to our adult session. As part of his therapy he had taken up swimming and could stay under water for two full minutes. One afternoon he was the only person who wanted to go swimming. Our Water Safety Instructor, camp nurse, and another certified life-guard all went to our small swimming hole. John had been swimming out and back to the dock. After two minutes he would surface, take a break, flirt with the nurse and swim the lap again using just his legs and good arm. Ten Mile Lake was notorious for being dark green caused by rampant algae. When he went under the water just a few inches he could not be seen. He simply went under on another lap and did not come up.

I had left camp to wrap up our business accounts in town. It was the only day the entire summer I had left. Danny was left in charge of the camp. He called the Sheriff, but before they arrived he found the camper and administered mouth to mouth. It was too late. John had passed.

All of the Easter Seal family felt the loss. Mush said he would drive down from Portland to tell his family. In his early sixties, I think he was feeling rather fatherly, I was the same age as his youngest son. "That's my job," I said. Ardi and I left immediately for Florence.

He was hunched over a power mower. He looked like he already had the weight of the world on his shoulders. The old tan pants, tan shirt and a tan baseball cap looked like something he probably wore to work. I steeled my courage. I would only add to his burdens.

"Mr. Metcalf, I'm Bob Ferguson the director of Camp Easter Seal," I said as I reached to shake his hand.

Before I could utter the most difficult words of my life, he asked "What's happened?"

"John was swimming, like he loved to do, and we're not sure what happened. He went under the water and never came up. My brother found him and gave him mouth-to-mouth resuscitation, but it was too late. Since he was such a good swimmer we think he had an aneurysm. There was no struggle or panic he just slipped away without suffering. (Aneurysms are quite common among patients with brain injuries.)

His brimming tears spilled over. "Maybe it's for the best," he said. "He was so unhappy with his life. Just before camp he said that he 'was only half a person.' You know, he was a star basketball player and a decorated Vietnam veteran. He was just so frustrated with his handicap."

"If your wife is home, would you like me to tell her?"

"She's in the house, it's going to tear her apart she loved him so. She's the one that got him into swimming you know. He was so proud that he could stay under water so long. But I'll be goin' in now to tell her, thank you for coming."

Kids should not die before their parents. That should be one of God's rules. My thinking was clouded with sorrow for this man, but I uttered those inane, useless, but required words, "If there is anything I can do, please don't hesitate to call on me," and handed him my card.

As he walked across the half mowed lawn, his shoulders were more stooped than before. They had twice lost their only child.

At camp we held a memorial service in our outdoor chapel. A Colossal Myrtle Wood tree grew above an embankment that formed a natural "grotto." Giant Sword Ferns hanging over the bank added a beauty that Hollywood couldn't match in its finest hour. It was one of our favorite spots to show visitors. The towering tree, and ancient plants commanded a reverence I have never known in any other chapel. It was a heartrending, tears flowing service. It brought closure to the camp. After the service we had our usual activities. That night we had the best dance ever. Our lives were re-started.

With the exception of the tragedy, the summer was magnificent. The Special Focus session proved to be a gigantic achievement. A few of my articles were accepted in *Camping* magazine and directors from other camps for the handicapped were noticing our willingness to try new programs. By any standard, it was a success.

***

Directing the camp was only half of the job. Fundraising, asking for money for nothing in return, was the other half and the hardest part of the job. After being gone all summer at camp, in September I began traveling to each of the thirty six counties in Oregon. At each stop I gave a speech about Easter Seals and our summer camp.

The philanthropic sorority of Sigma Alpha Epsilon adopted Easter Seals as their national project. They were a gigantic help and nearly all of our county chairmen came from their ranks.

To get the cheapest mailing rates we would box our brochures, with return envelopes and send them via UPS to each county. A significant logistical chore. The sororities would stuff the envelopes and mail them from their zip code. This gave us the cheapest bulk rates. It was a monumental task and their help was essential so my job of keeping them in the fold was paramount. I always made sure to mention any camper from their town or county. I also asked if they knew someone who could use a wheelchair or maybe a child who might like to go to camp.

The travels took me from Astoria to Lakeview with side trips to Drewsey, Shaniko, and Dufur to drop off a coin canister at the local grocery store. Most camp directors hated the fundraising part of the job. I loved it. Both jobs together were like a dinner of "steak and lobster," the mingled flavors were magnificent!

The only real part of the job I disliked was moving heavy boxes in my coat and tie on a regular basis. Okay, I was also the office "gopher." Since my schedule was flexible I would be told to "go-for this or go-for that." These were merely annoyances in a job I relished. Even your dream job will have irritations. Get over them. They make the fun parts more fun.

One thing I had learned about public speaking, if you emotionally stir the audience, your contributions increase exponentially. With no pangs of conscience, I milked it by closing each presentation with this anonymous poem, allegedly written by a ten year old boy.

Crippled Billy

They call me "Crippled Billy,"
And I guess that is my name,
But the crippled part is not my heart
My legs are all that's lame.

The Billy part is me sir
Just a lively wiggling boy,
'cause a happy face doesn't need a brace
When bandaged up with joy.

The inside isn't crippled,
That's the Billy part you know,
Just the body part and not the heart
Is all that didn't grow.

    Of course I used dramatic pauses and voice inflections to get the tears flowing in the crowd. It always meant a good fundraising day. Shame on me! Hey, it was for a good cause.

    Relationships with staff and campers continue to this day, but mostly live in our memories of an incredible era. As life happens, I occasionally run into campers and staff for a rousing reunion in the grocery line or at a Saturday Market. Then there is the inevitable obituary that reminds me of how Colossal my life has been. The following 2012, Oregonian article has been edited.

*Ed. note: Melvin Bush, well known to Southwest Portland residents as the man who sold coffee from his wheelchair around the Portland State University campus, died from complications related to cerebral palsy. He was 64. **A funeral was held on Tuesday.** Former Oregonian reporter Spencer Heinz wrote this feature about Bush and his daily routine in 2003.*

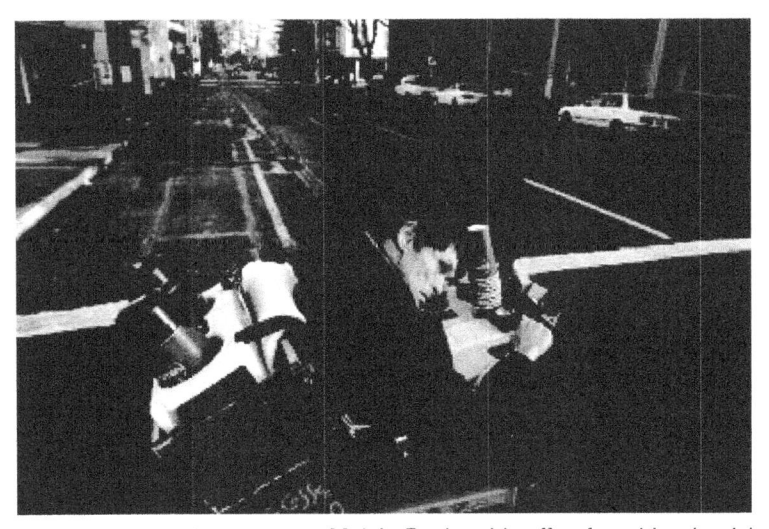

Michael Lloyd/The Oregonian/2003 Melvin Bush sold coffee from his wheelchair because he wanted a job.

HAVE COFFEE, WILL TRAVEL

He sells coffee. A lot of people sell coffee. About every corner has coffee. Then again, has anyone thought of selling coffee between the corners? Melvin Bush has. He has because he wanted a job.

He works out of a wheelchair that he maneuvers with a joystick. His chair is rigged with a wooden box for two pots of coffee, plus cups up front and a fastened-down clock. It times his daily circuit that others mark their mornings by. He's downtown Portland's only traveling barista.

He sells at his regular stops and to passers-by. He has the job because his skills range, "from total dependability and a brilliant mind to a knack and drive for selling," said his employer.

Born in 1955 in Eugene, OR. with cerebral palsy, Bush cannot walk. He has limited use of his hands. He is not able to enunciate the full range of words. He fills the space with intonations of "yes" and "no" and "oh yeah," plus the bracingly sarcastic, "Oh yeah. Right!"

His job did not happen by chance. He spent his younger years in the former Fairview Training Center for those with disabilities. He wanted out, and he became one of the first residents to persuade officials, in the 1970s, to let him move into a group home and later into an apartment alone. He lived, jobless, on Social Security disability and food stamps.

The severity of his cerebral palsy made him unemployable, at least in traditional ways of thinking. He could have continued living on disability funds. But he wanted a job for the same reasons that other people want jobs: a paycheck, meeting others, contributing, having somewhere to go each day.

Last fall he went to the state's Vocational Rehabilitation office to ask for help finding work downtown. David Kern, job developer, accepted the mission. He knocked on the doors of downtown coffee shops and restaurants.

Managers said they would get back to him if something opened up. Then came a breakthrough. Julia Harshberger, cafe manager of Seattle's Best Coffee at Southwest Sixth Avenue near Mill Street, asked Bush in for an interview.

He did well. She hired him at the standard start of $6.90 an hour. She snapped his picture, posted it with snapshots of other employees on the cafe's "Wall of Fame," worked with agencies to outfit his chair with coffee-selling gear and launched him onto downtown streets.

He starts at 8 a.m., stops a block down for Mike, the parking lot man. Mike was not a coffee drinker before meeting Melvin. Mike says, Melvin sold him cup number one.

For newcomers, Melvin leans toward his serving-table card. "Hi – My name is Melvin, if you'd like me to come to your office every day, I can put you on my route. Please call Julia at 503-273-9689 to set it up." New patrons learn by watching. Regulars pour their own, mark the inventory sheet, drop cash in the crockpot and make their own change.

Most days he swings by the DMV, the American Automobile Association, Wells Fargo, U.S. Bank, Portland State University's Extended Studies building, Basha's Mediterranean Cuisine, the Fire Bureau's Engine 4, spots in between.

"He's the greased lightning around here," his boss says. "He's fulfilled all of the ideals that this company holds onto."

As Melvin ends another refilling stop, one of the cafe patrons, Tom the urban studies man, steps out of the cafe's counter line.

"What," he asks gently, "is this all about, this wheelchair with coffee?" Melvin tips toward the sign that says, "Hi My name is Melvin." Three steps from the cafe's counter, Tom buys from Melvin. He takes a cup, tells Melvin "thanks," says "I'll be back again tomorrow."-- *Spencer Heinz*

One of my great regrets is that for nine years I never hustled down town to get a cup of Jo from Mel. There seemed to be plenty of time. I was shocked to read his obituary. Another opportunity slipped through my grasp. I vow that I will never again waste an opportunity. But I will. I'm human, but I'm putting it in writing!

I went to his service expecting to see some of the old gang from Easter Seal. There were over 100 people. They were all from his business as a wheelchair barista. Melvin epitomized the independence we were encouraging at camp. In a small way, I have no doubt we contributed to his self-reliance. When I was in college, I once visited Mel in Fairview. He immediately went to their toy box and got out a plastic bat and ball like we had at camp. I began to pitch to him. It was as though we had never left. Between the concerted efforts of his parents, Fairview State Hospital, Easter Seal Society, and numerous others, Mel found a level of independence and touched the lives of many. The epitaph in his memorial program says it all.

Melvin Lee Bush November 10, 1947 - July 11, 2012

That Man Is A Success

Who has lived well, laughed often

and loved much;

Who has gained the respect of

intelligent men and the love of children;

Who has filled his niche

and accomplished his task;

Who leaves the world better

than he found it, whether by an improved

poppy, a perfect poem, or a rescued soul;

Who never lacked appreciation of

earth's beauty or failed to express it;

Who looked for the best in others and gave the best he had.

That man is a success.

Chapter 2

Business Stories

(The following was an exercise assigned in a memoir writing class. The prompt was "The Fork." Most class members wrote something about being jabbed in one way or another. It was a fun assignment. I encourage you to grab a sheet of paper and write about your "Fork.")

The Fork

By Bob Ferguson

"I came to a fork in the road...so I took it." Yogi Berra

President Nixon had announced an expansion of Lyndon Johnson's "Great Society." The poverty level for a single person was now $10,000 dollars a year. If you had a family, it was much lower. Our family of four easily qualified. After four years as the director of Camp Easter Seal, I had apparently worked hard enough to achieve poverty. It seemed a bit short for a college graduate who had, four years earlier, left the Marine Corps as a Captain earning $16,000 a year with superb benefits. I had no chance of getting close to that figure as a camp director for a non-profit organization. I loved directing a camp for handicapped kids, but "Charity begins at home."

On the radio Ray Orbison was crooning to his "Pretty Woman." At thirty years of age, the tunes of my youth were now on the oldies station. The odometer on our '69 Impala had turned over 100,000 miles shortly before I wheeled into the crowded parking lot of the Welfare Office. Surrounded by a sea of clunkers, the Chevy looked pretty good.

"Take a number," the sign read. So I did. After the protracted wait that is required at any governmental agency, my number was finally called. The questions were simple, "What is your household income?" We were old school and Ardi stayed home with the kids. The numbers were so low the math was easy. "Ten thousand, nine hundred a year," I said. "How many children," asked the matronly lady. She was wearing black, frumpy shoes beneath the hem of a long pink, well used, floral dress that fell short of covering grotesque, baggy nylons. "Two," I said. "How much do you have in savings?" She asked. "Three thousand," I announced proudly.

For the first time in the interview, over the top of thick, horned rimmed glasses, she looked at me before delivering her verdict. "You can get $50 dollars a month in food stamps, but you have too much in savings to get any salary assistance." "What if I buy a new car with my savings?" I asked. "Well, then you would qualify for $150 in food stamps and some salary assistance." She had just offered me the "Cadillac Clause" in the welfare system. Spend your savings to get on the public dole. But what the heck, no system is perfect.

Directing Camp Easter Seal was the fulfillment of a dream that I had worked towards since volunteering as a counselor. The four camp years had been a special time, but I was now ready to move on to another challenge and...lots more money. I began grabbing the Sunday Oregonian and circling items in the "Job

Opportunities" column. I leaned toward sales jobs with a salary, plus commission. Being a stockbroker appealed to me. I went on a few job interviews, took a lot of tests and was offered several jobs, but on commission only. With a family of four, I needed security and the bigger companies offered what I needed. I interviewed and landed a job as a stockbroker with Merrill Lynch, Pierce, Fenner, and Smith.

My thirst to be the camp director had been slaked. Mush, knew that financially I needed to move on and he wished me well. I left with good feelings. I've stayed in touch with many of those friends we made while sitting around a campfire singing "This Land is Your Land." I kept track of Mush until his passing.

Mother Merrill, as we called the company, took care of us. The salary was the same as I had at Easter Seals, but the commissions would quickly triple that figure. All I had to do was work hard at selling. They hired brokers from two backgrounds; those who were *from* money and those who were *hungry* for money.

The training was outrageously excellent. I would study two weeks at the beautiful downtown Portland office in the tall Georgia Pacific building. Then I would travel to The Big Apple for twelve weeks training at the Merrill Lynch headquarters. I would live with two other trainees and it was all on the company dime. A few guys had MBA degrees and they all agreed that it was like a mini-MBA program. We sat for the exams of the New York Stock Exchange, the Chicago Board of Options, the National Association of Security Dealers, and the American Stock Exchange. We knew our stuff. Surprisingly, there were no classes on sales.

The stock market had been attaining new highs every day and had just broken 1,000. I was missing out on all the action! My licenses came in the mail on nearly the same day the Arab Oil Embargo began. We had to wait in line to get gas and people complained about the ridiculous price of fifty cents per gallon. The stock market dropped like a rock from 1,100 to the 300 level and the volume plummeted from 20 million shares a day to less than ten million. The office conference calls with New York stressed that in every down market there is opportunity. I began selling "undervalued" stocks that were not petroleum based. If a customer called and asked about GM I would ask "Are you thinking of buying or selling that stock?" If the answer was "buying" I would give them a good reason to buy. My commission would be 8½%. If they were thinking of selling, my spiel would be "Why don't we take the profit on that stock and then buy XYZ stock?" I made 17% on a sell and buy transaction! To my everlasting shame, I was good at it, but I began to have trouble sleeping.

Merrill developed their own income fund containing high dividend stocks. We were asked to sell the company's Lionel D. Edie Income Fund to all of our customers. There would be a contest with cash prizes. I led the company in new accounts, but was blown away by the *big hitters* in the volume category. One of my new accounts was a lady who had called in while I was manning the lunch time phone duty. She asked "What do you have for income?" Super Salesman was all over it. She had $180,000 held in a trust account at a bank. Funds held in trust at a bank are something like a mutual fund. They are co-mingled with other client's money and offer a very low rate of return, but they are not guaranteed by the FDIC as she mistakenly thought. She took her money out of the bank and put it into the Lionel D. Edie fund. I made $15,300. It would be a sweet Christmas.

On Christmas Eve, at about 8:30 PM I got a call from my client. She was in tears. Her attorney convinced her that I had put her in an investment vehicle that was too risky for her. She now wanted to put the money back into the trust at the bank. Oh, did I mention, her attorney, being the trustee was paid a fee. I didn't argue too hard because I would make another $15,300 on the sale.

Maybe it was the spirit of the Season, her attorney may have been Grinch, but I did my own soul searching. I found that I was more concerned about my retirement, than my client's. I would make the story of any stock work so I made as much money as possible. It was a far cry from singing "Kumbaya" around the campfire with handicapped kids. It wasn't me. I had internalized the adage I had used many times in my fundraising programs "*Takers* eat better, but *Givers* sleep better." I needed some Z's…bad. I again turned to the "Job Opportunities" column.

✶✶✶

Do It Yourself!

The Edman Furniture store was a landmark in Eugene. Located off the north end of the Ferry Street Bridge it was the epitome of a successful, family owned business. It was founded by Lloyd Edman Sr. and continues through the third generation. My good friend, Babe Edman, his younger siblings Steve, and Mary took over the reins when Lloyd Senior retired. It is where I got my first taste of business and politics.

A few Saturdays during high school the store needed a little extra help delivering furniture. Babe would ask me to fill in. I jumped at the chance because Lloyd Sr. paid well. He also dispensed his Minnesota work ethic, "work hard and you'll always have a job." I took that not only as an admonishment to give him a full day's work, but also as good advice.

Like most small business enterprises, Lloyd risked his own money, worked long hours, six days a week, and involved his entire family. He railed at taxes, was disgusted with welfare, and was therefore, of course, a staunch Republican. It was my first introduction to real-world politics.

On the other side of the coin – he was generous to the community and Central Lutheran Church, where he was a main benefactor and leader. In the back of my mind I had developed the idea that someday I might like to own my own business.

Years later, during my hiatus from Merrill, Babe and I got together. He told me to call Neil Richardson of Richardson Sports. Neil was looking for a salesman to represent his sporting goods distributing business which warehoused athletic goods. "Socks and jocks, hats and bats," is how I referred to the business. He hired me part-time, paid me a small wage, put gas in the tank of our Buick Roadmaster, Station Wagon which Ardi's parents had given to us. It was old, but held all the samples I needed to schlep.

My job was to present/sell Neil's products to the smaller sporting goods stores, like Caplan's Sporting Goods, Portland Athletic, Stottlemeyer Athletic in Yakima, Athletic Supply in Seattle, and every Mom and Pop operation in Oregon and Washington.

When I got up in the morning I had to read the sports page, visit a few stores, talk local sports, show my wares, take orders, and that was it. Each sales call lasted no more than an hour, but I often had to wait while the owner helped a customer. The calls were made in the morning. Store owners were busy the minute kids got out of school. That was great for me, I could be home for practice of whatever sport I was coaching at that time.

One day Neil showed me a plastic soccer shin-guard. We thought we could make a better one. For a full year I delved into injection molding, types of foam, packaging, marketing, and how patents are not always a good thing. It was a Colossal learning experience. After the research, we pooled our money and the Richardson Shin-Guard was born. It was plastic with a cantilevered, shock-absorbing center that protected the shin, foam backing added to the safety, and little pointed sock-grabbers held it in place without cumbersome straps. The first pair cost us $12,000 dollars. The second pair was .05 cents. We sold them for $1.50 so the stores could sell them for $3.00 dollars and make a "Keystone" profit. We doubled our money within the first year. It was the best on the market.

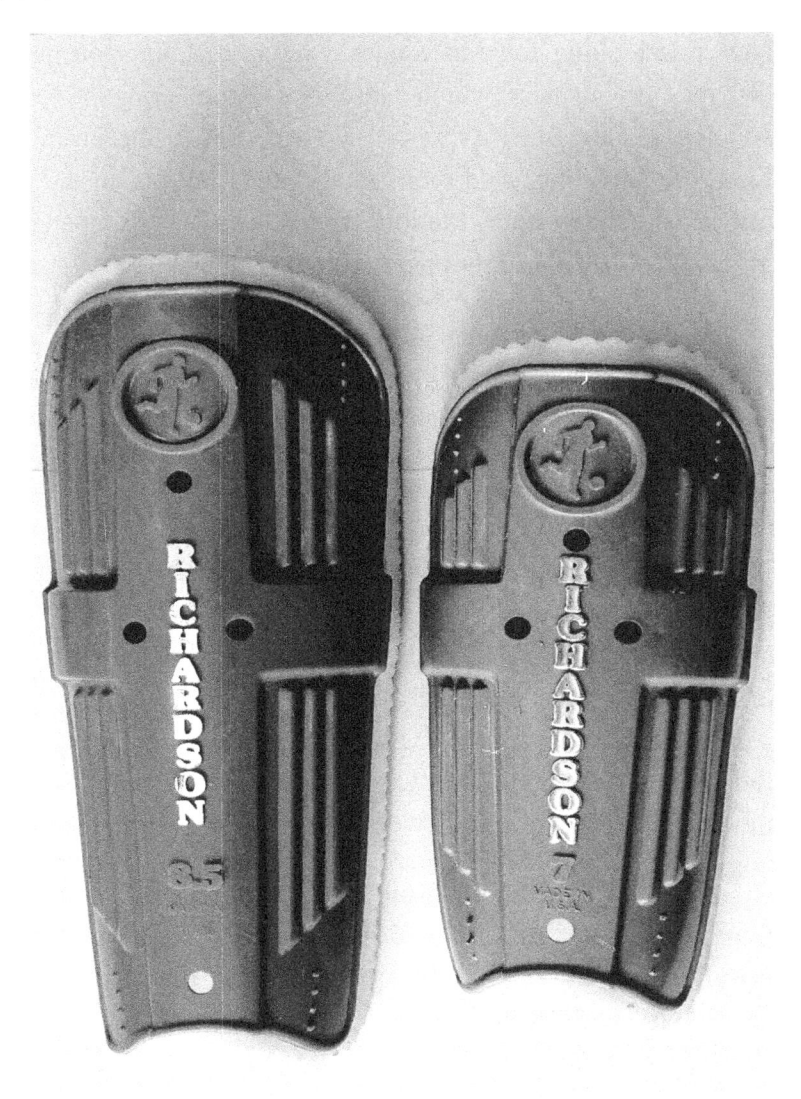

It was a fun job, but Neil had a son who would soon be coming into the business and I needed to make a living wage. In addition to business partners we were friends. It was awkward, but he bought me out of the shin-guard business and helped me get started as a manufacturer's representative. It was a win-win for both of us.

To keep food on the table at home while I was building the "Bob Ferguson and Associates," business, I taught management classes through Portland Community College. It was a class I created and pitched to the school. It was so much fun that I did it for several years and it paid enough to cover our essentials.

The companies I represented did not require warehousing so my only investment was in samples and most of them were free. The business flourished. People who had teased me about the "and Associates" title on my business card knew I was having the last laugh. But all good things come to an end. After about ten years, school budgets were cut, kids had to pay to play sports, and Nike was giving away what I was trying to sell. To survive, my dream business had to morph into another entity.

One of the lines we represented was King Louie, a line of bowling shirts and baseball type sports jackets. At a time when the sport of bowling was dying on the vine, one of our best sellers came along. It was a satin jacket, in bright team colors with knit stripes around the collar and cuffs. Team sales were relatively small orders but we began to get large orders from screen-printers and embroiderers for company events.

This new "decorator" market opened up another door and we walked through it. (I use the term "we." Every small business is usually a family operation. Ardi kept the books and received a wage. My kids helped me at the shows, ran the garage sales, and got to live at our house. Rachel eventually came to work in the business. The marketing and sales experience has added to the type of classes she is qualified to instruct in her teaching career.)

The decorator market let us morph into the "Ad-Specialty" market where we sold CPS – Cheap Plastic Stuff. We were among a handful of reps selling to the team, decorator, and Ad-Specialty markets. As the first two dwindled, the Ad-Specialty market dwarfed our previous sales and our net commissions sky-rocketed. Our customers in this market were called "Distributors." They were the people actually selling to Microsoft, Weyerhaeuser the local auto dealer, and other small businesses. I was the epitome of the middle-man and loved it!

In addition to being a fun job that rewarded creativity in sales, being my own boss, working from a home-office, it afforded me a chance to coach my kids. My sales calls were made in the morning and I was on the soccer or baseball field just after the kids got out of school. Ditto the basketball court. My coaching endeavors now total about thirty years, all pee-wee sports. Easily some of the best years of our lives. We have attended the weddings of some of the kids and the "Celebration of Life" for a few of my fellow coaches.

It is a character flaw, but I seem to get over-involved in everything so I became the president of most leagues, as well as the Cub Master. There were, of course, the overly competitive type of parents, but they did not diminish my experience one iota.

The busiest people were the best volunteers and one to whom every Portlander owes a debt of gratitude is Carol Hundeby. I digress a little to tell this story.

Carol called me one day to see if I would coach the kindergarten/first grade soccer team. I had been coaching Little League baseball for several years before my kids were old enough to play, but this was the first sport where I could coach our oldest son, Robb. I said yes, then went to a sporting goods store to buy a book about soccer. There were none. I went to the library and checked out a book on this foreign sport I wasn't quite sure I would like.

The field is called a "pitch and players can "tackle" each other. So far so good. Drawing diagrams to show the player's positions, a few warm up drills, and a scrimmage at the end of practice would be enough to get us started.

Parents were delighted to drop off their kids at the school. As organized as Carol and I were, the practice quickly devolved into a kick-and-run session. We were charting new territory. The ninety minutes passed quickly, the kids had fun, but as a coach, I was in way over my head. No turning back. We muddled through the first few practices. Our goalie, fullbacks, mid-fielders, and forwards had somewhat learned their positions. We were set for the big game on Saturday.

Once the ball was kicked it was a mad scramble of what looked like a bunch of bumble bees kicking at the ball. Parents who had never seen a practice or had any idea about positions on a soccer field, still exhorted their little bundles of joy to "Get in there and kick that ball." Despite our best efforts to educate the parents and players, the last game of the season looked exactly like the first, it was bumble-bee soccer. Colossal!

Every practice, every game was so special that I called the park department to find other teams in town to play a practice game. The park department didn't know there were ANY soccer teams in Portland. Carol Hundeby had organized all of the teams at six elementary schools by herself. She simply thought it was such a "...neat game..."

Our small group of teams had about 150 players. All of the teams were co-ed and were strictly recreational in design. During the off-season, Carol set up a meeting with the Park Department. She, myself, and one other parent met with the Portland officials. We wrote a rule book, reserved various city parks, and she singlehandedly contacted most of the elementary schools in the Portland Metro area. The next year there were 3,500 kids playing soccer. The following year there were adult leagues and about 25,000 people playing soccer in the metro area.

A few years ago the Oregonian was extoling the virtues of Mick Hoban for starting youth soccer in Portland. No way! Carol Hundeby quietly started the movement! The Portland Park Department, along with myself and Mr. Jubitz of truck stop fame, are witnesses to the beginnings. Mick was a Johnny-come-lately.

A memoir is about the only place where you get to set the record straight. While coaching the pee-wee sports of our kids I ran into a lot of good people, like Carol, who did the right thing solely because it was "the right thing to do." And in later years it was a real boon for the Richardson Shin-guard. Thank you Carol Hundeby! Myself and the entire prolific, Portland soccer scene are in your debt!

***

Paul Zidell

(A Memoir Class assignment with the prompt "Bamboozled.")

Bad people are not dreadful all of the time and good people are not forever angelic, but Paul Zidell was pure evil 24/7. It has always puzzled me why talented people, like him, spend so much time conniving to separate others from their hard earned cash when they could use that same time and talent to build respectable fortunes. Maybe it's the adrenaline rush they get by outsmarting the naïve or a sick pleasure from devising a diabolical plot that operates an eighth of an inch inside the law. It was a legal scheme to be sure and a profitable plot indeed, but Paul Zidell's plan wreaked such devastation upon families it could only end in ruin.

Dressed in a Joseph Abboud, three piece, Glenn Plaid, suit standing in front of his beautiful display of athletic socks at the Sporting Goods Manufacturer's Association Show, in Atlanta, Georgia, Paul Zidell was the picture of success. His light blue shirt picked up the subtle blue stripes in his gray suit. The red silk tie harmonized with his expensive black wing-tip shoes and sculpted an image of luxurious accomplishment. There was no clue that a deadly snake lay hidden inside such posh trappings.

The plan was simple; I buy $250 worth of well packaged sample socks, pre-sell them to my customers and then place the combined orders with Paul. The socks would be shipped to my warehouse AKA our large, unfinished basement. Then all I had to do was load up our ginormous, fake wood paneled, '68 Buick Roadmaster, station wagon and deliver them.

I wanted to dress like Paul. I wanted as much money as Paul. I wanted to exude business confidence like Paul. But there was one catch; I would have to order $100,000 dollars in goods on a Letter of Credit to get started.

He must have been laughing inside, as I begged him to let me start with less. He told me I was a "smooth talker" and with feigned reluctance, he agreed to let me into his program, while adding a surcharge for a smaller quantity. I was in Seventh Heaven, but I had just made a deal with El Diablo (The Devil.)

The band around the sample socks was emblazoned with the colors of green, yellow and black. The logo was a low flying black duck with the stylized name of Duxx wrapped around the tube socks. They were constructed with a 100% cotton foot and a nylon top for stronger hold and more vibrant athletic team colors. They were a high quality product for an average price. Selling them to sporting goods stores was like taking candy from a baby. I would soon be rich! Steak and lobster would replace burgers and fries.

After only one week, sales were so good I had to increase my order from $10,000 to $16,000, but our life's savings stopped at $10,000. Along with a group of friends we had formed an investment club, which had an extra $6,000 in cash. I pitched them for $6,000. They bought in for a percent of my nearly guaranteed profits. It would be fun to make money for my friends.

A Letter of Credit is like a cashier's check purchased from a bank; in this case, the now defunct First National Bank. It is a standard way of doing business with companies located in foreign countries. There are stipulations that the goods must be shipped before the money exchanges hands. It was only slightly unusual that a domestic company would have such a requirement. So, I raced right down to the bank and shelled out $16,000, plus a $100 bank fee to get the socks shipped to my rapidly expanding empire.

While waiting for my socks to come home to roost, I continued selling from my sample kit. I had pre-booked another $16,000 for a total of $32,000, but I had no operating capital to buy more goods. I was tapped out. I would have to quickly turn the in-route socks to cash. I offered customers a nice discount if they would pay Cash on Delivery. Most of the accounts were long time customers with whom I had done solid business with for several years. They knew I was honest and letting them in on a ground floor opportunity.

The big cardboard cartons filled my basement. They were unmarked as to contents so each one would have to be opened to sort out the colors and get them quickly delivered in the Roadmaster. I carefully opened the first box. The socks were packaged by the dozen in a thin gray box, with twenty boxes to a carton. It was an inconvenience that the boxes and cartons were not labeled as to color and style, but they all had to be opened anyway. I eagerly flipped the top off of the box. "What the…these aren't the colors I ordered! Why would he send me tennis socks with pink stripes when I ordered all athletic colors like purple and gold? Look at this; it's even a different label and not nearly the quality of my samples!" I yelled at my wife. My stomach churned, the blood drained from my head at the instant realization that I had been bamboozled. I was drowning.

I sliced open the other cartons. The colors were a mishmash of tan and brown stripes, light blue and royal, all fashion colors. They were totally unacceptable for the team dealers to whom I had pre-sold school colors! These socks were not even close to the quality of the goods I had been showing to the dealers. I was sick!

Paul's voice on his recorder sounded pleasant. I knew there had to be a mistake that could be corrected. I left a detailed message of my problem. I was very concerned, but not alarmed—that came later. My last message on Ziddel's recorder indicated I would soon be hiring a lawyer if he didn't call back.

The First National Bank said my money in the LOC was collected the day the goods were shipped. The banker said "You should have made your LOC contingent upon the inspection of the goods."

"I didn't know I could and you were paid $100 dollars for your expertise. It was your fiduciary responsibility to inform me of the pitfalls," I accused.

Smirking, he said "So sue us." We both knew a lawsuit would cost more than the money I was trying to recover.

At thirty three—I was a failure and flat broke. I panicked and sold the majority of the socks to a reputable dealer on consignment. They went bankrupt. Again it was The First National Bank that closed down the store and took possession of my goods. My explanation that my socks were not the store's property fell on deaf ears. Again I heard "So sue us."

"You get to keep your house and one car," the attorney said during my free, fifteen minute consultation.

"What would it do to my credit?" I asked.

"We just deal with the law," he said.

Through garage sales and a few dealers I was able to sell the remaining socks, but I lost every dime of savings and $3,000 of my friends' money. I was humiliated. My soul was crushed.

The SGMA sporting goods show rolled around again and I went to Chicago. I thought about mugging Ziddel every time he went to the men's room. I laughed as I pictured him being so afraid to take a leak that his bladder would fill up and he'd explode like a water balloon.

He was wearing the same suit and tie and was mesmerizing a crowd just like he had captivated me. The deadly viper was striking again. I walked to the front of the crowd.

"Hi Bob, it's great to see you again," he said like he was welcoming a much loved relative. He had more guts than a burglar just to show up.

"Well, I'm surprised you're here. I thought you'd be out of business by now from the way you bilk people out of their life's savings," I said.

"Bob you got every pair of socks you ordered and your bad business practices aren't my fault." He had a gift of being able to make people see what he wanted them to see.

The crowd gave me reviled looks reserved for the dirty homeless guy asking for spare change for food when you know he'll buy wine. I was belittled…but not beaten. As anger filled my body making my ears warm, I gathered my courage. I would cut off the head of this snake before he could inject his venom into more people.

"One of his requirements is that you put up a Letter of Credit. Then he ships factory seconds or overruns that are nothing close to the quality that he's showing you today," I said. The small crowd's looks of disdain changed to amused interest.

"Bob, it was your own business practices that caused you to fail and that's slander, I'll sue you," he said with all the guile he could muster.

"If it's true, it's not slander and I would welcome getting you in court. Here's my card for anyone who wants to talk to me," I retorted.

Everyone in the crowd took a card as they left. Several times throughout the three days of the show I repeated my performance. When Ziddel would see me coming he would end his little presentations, but not before I chased the people down and gave them my story. Ziddel did not have a booth at the next show that year. He knew I would be there to expose him as a charlatan.

One of my fellow bilkees who lost his entire retirement savings said that he was "connected" and could make sure "Ziddel wouldn't be doing any more business." I thought he meant by taking him to court. To this day I am bemused by his comment; in less than a year, Paul Ziddel improved the human gene pool by dying of a well-deserved heart attack. It has crossed my mind that he died of "Natural Causes" that were somehow helped along?

The saddest part of this story is not the disgrace I felt or the money I lost. I call that tuition for "The School of Hard Knocks." It's a private school; you have to be stupid to get in, but you are a whole lot smarter by graduation time. I financially recovered and my friends are still my good friends. But my decision making capabilities were crippled for years. It made me overly cautious and afraid to invest. I said "no" to one of my sock customers who asked me to invest in his little company called "Blue Ribbon Sports," which later became known as…Nike.

***

Judgment

(A Prompt For Another Memoir Class Assignment)

by Bob Ferguson

The Bando brothers would have been dead-ringers to star in any of the "God Father" movies. Lou and Sal Bando had thick black hair, olive skin and were movie star handsome. They always dressed to the nines, talked about their country club, and were money flaunting, high rollers who left me terribly embarrassed at a national sales meeting back in '73. But not as badly as I, myself mortified a few people.

We were manufacturers' representatives for the King Louie Apparel company. Our job was to show jacket and shirt samples and leave catalogs with screen print and embroidery shops. In the trade they were called decorators. They, in turn sold, to the buying public, known in the business as "end users." Each rep was assigned a geographical territory of several states and received a commission from all of the customers who bought goods within their territory.

The Bandos were an anomaly within the industry. They were not only reps selling to the decorator trade, but they owned the largest screen print and embroidery business in Chicago and also sold directly to end users competing against their own customers. So how could they get away with such a conflict of interest? They were by far, King Louie's biggest customer. Their customer base included nearly every union in Chicago and Detroit. I can't say they were definitely "connected," but they were certainly "linked."

After the '73 annual sales meeting, my fellow rep, John Bell Senior, and I were approached by the Bandos to share a limousine ride with them to the airport. They convinced us that if we split the forty dollar cost between the four of us we could ride in style and it would cost about the same as a cab. They were smooth. We bought in.

The brothers had won the salesmen of the year trophy at the awards banquet the previous night. As we boarded the limo the next morning an adoring crowd had gathered. As I sat in the limo, I basked in the reflected glory of the Bando's success. I waved goodbye to the doting crowd with the practiced, circular motions of a Rose Parade Queen.

The salesmen of the year were dropped off first. They jumped out of the limo, grabbed their bags, and ran through revolving doors. There was no hand shake, or "See you next year," kind of farewell. More importantly, there was no twenty bucks for the limo driver! I began to sweat. As usual, I was almost broke. When divided by four, the forty dollar cost was fair. But split between only two of us, it was more money than I had in my pockets.

My terminal was next. Stammering, I opened my wallet and I swear moths flew out. The ten dollar bill I thought I had in it was gone. Suddenly I remembered buying the Bandos drinks the night before to congratulate them on their trophy and I had forgotten to borrow some cash from a another rep. I was utterly flat broke and I had no credit card. On the lives of my four children, I swore to John that I would send him my share if he would catch the limo bill. What else could he do? "I've got it covered, but I won't hold my breath" John said as I sheepishly shook his hand.

When I got home I immediately got a twenty dollar bill from my wife's purse. To add some levity, I put it in a humorous envelope a friend had given me. I called John Senior and left a message on his recorder that a crisp, "double sawbuck" had been mailed and he would receive it shortly. I had not only paid my portion of the limo fare, but also ten bucks for one of the free-loading Bandos. My job was done. My conscience was clear.

John Bell Senior was a humble, religious man. He was out of place at sales meetings. They invariably overflowed with testosterone and blue jokes. Senior was a church deacon and had gone on missions to build schools in Africa. This was his last sales meeting before John Junior would take over the business.

I could not possibly have foreseen that his church was having a special "African Schools" offering the Sunday after Senior received my envelope. It was impossible for me to predict that instead of using an offering envelope, Senior would simply cross out my name on the return address and drop the unopened envelope into the offering plate. Thinking that it actually contained a twenty dollar bill took an act of faith in itself.

My still unopened envelope was passed from the church treasurer, to the church secretary who gave it unopened to the church pastor. Tongues wagged and rumors flew.

A year later I ran into John Junior at a trade show and he couldn't wait to tell me "The rest of the Story." "That Monday after you sent my dad the twenty bucks he got a call from the pastor asking if everything was okay at home. Dad says everything is great and then the pastor asks if he can drop by the house for a few minutes. Of course Dad says sure." Junior was now warming to his topic.

"After talking about nothing the pastor gives my dad your still unopened envelope and leaves. Dad had no idea what was going on with the preacher until he turns over your envelope and sees the red lettering on the back, 'Confidential Medical Information: Your Herpes Test Results Are Enclosed,'" Knowing the punch line, we both had tears in our eyes from laughing.

The twenty dollar bill did find its way into the offering plate and John Senior should be nominated for Sainthood. In the Bible classes he taught he used my novelty envelope as a prop for teaching Mathew 7:1 "Judge not, that ye be not judged."

In addition to the tons of laughter this story has provided, I learned three important lessons. First, be wary of high rollers, they may be steam rollers. Second, always make sure you've got enough money for cab fare or you might get taken for a ride. Finally, never send anything through the mail you wouldn't want your pastor to read.

Chapter 3

Family Stories

The Sermon

At nearly ninety years old, Lester never held back. Why should he? He was given to occasionally telling a good story that reminded us of our human nature—no matter where he was, even if it interrupted a church sermon. Lester's small,stooped figure rose from the third row pew he had sat in for decades of Sundays.

"I've got a good one for you Del," he said interrupting pastor Del Keller in mid-sentence.

Chuckles rippled through the congregation. Pastor Del had been preaching about "Giving God the Glory for all things." The flock awaited Lester's enlightening words.

"I know you've got a good one for us Lester," Del said giving us his customary big grin, as he respectfully deferred to Lester.

Lester commenced. *"A young preacher was given the task of rebuilding a dying church in a small farming community. He was fresh out of the seminary and eager to grow the flock. The young preacher wanted to get everybody back to the church. He stopped* beside a field a farmer was plowing and introduced himself. He said to the farmer, 'This is a beautiful crop of wheat.'"

'Thanks, I've done a lot of work to grow this wheat,' the farmer said.

'You mean you and God have done a lot to grow this beautiful crop,' the pastor said.

'Well, I cleared the stumps, plowed the field, and planted the seed.'

Lester O'Grady held the congregation in the palm of his hand. We all knew his story would give us a huge belly-laugh so we waited as he built the suspense to the punch line.

'Of course you did,' said the enthusiastic pastor, 'but God sent you the rain and the sun to make it grow, so like all things, it is really the Lord's work.'

'Well, I never looked at it quite like that, and I suppose there is a lesson somewhere in there,' said the farmer.

"The new pastor could feel the Lord working in the farmer," Lester said in a rising and lowering voice like a preacher at a tent revival.

Lester always gave his stories gusto. He used sweeping gestures to refer to the wheat field and a slow drawl when he was telling us what the farmer said.

"'So I couldn't of done all this without God's help, is that what you're saying?' The farmer asked."

"'Yes, yes, praise the Lord, that's exactly what I mean,' gushed the exuberant pastor."

"The farmer mulled it over and said," 'Well, I get what you're saying, but you should have seen this place when God had it all to himself...'"

Lester sat back down in the pew. The congregation roared. Lester had struck again. Del Keller, laughed long and hard. He ended his sermon with something like "Lester has given us the lesson for the day so why don't you all stay for coffee in the Fellowship Hall." It the liveliest and most fun coffee that I can ever remember.

It would be impossible for this scene to have taken place at one of the mega-service, all glass, cathedrals. You know the type; the pastor is a robe wearing, big-haired, high salaried preacher. Sooner or later, in every service, he will eventually preach about the evils of you keeping your hard earned money. But this was a small neighborhood church led by a baseball fanatic who coveted the Lesters in his congregation. This story is about Del Keller.

Many preachers seem unapproachable unless you have an unblemished past, carry a Bible at all times, and say a Blessing at every meal. But I first knew Del only as a nice guy who enjoyed baseball. We each coached a team of eight year olds, attended the coach's monthly meetings, and enjoyed the company of other men who loved sports, kids, and competition. And Del was a competitor—to a fault!

One sunny afternoon Del's team of eight and nine year olds was playing my team. The game ebbed back and forth with each team scoring lots of runs. We were ahead by one run in the last inning with Del's team at bat. It was one of those plays where the ball gets thrown all over the field, but we were able to make the last out at home plate and win the game. It was a dubious call made by a young volunteer umpire. Did I mention that Del loved to compete? Del would never directly accost the poor kid umpiring, but he threw his hat on the ground, stomped on it and said, "Even Ray Charles could see he was safe."

I couldn't contain my laughter, nor could the fans. Del was making a spectacle of himself. He quickly realized we were laughing at him and he profusely apologized to the ump, all of the fans, and me.

"What do you do for a living?" I asked after his apology.

"I'm afraid I'm too embarrassed to tell you," he said as he brushed the dust off of his freshly trampled hat.

"Well you apologized to everybody and you had a sense of humor about your complaint so it's all forgotten," I said.

"It's embarrassing because I'm the pastor at the Methodist Church up on the hill by the blinking yellow light," he said.

I'm sure my resurgence of laughter didn't quell his embarrassment.

"Any guy who can stomp on his little league hat on Saturday and preach on Sunday sounds like my kind of preacher," I said.

After the season was over, Ardi and I made it up to the little church on the hill. Along with a few others, Del acknowledged us as visitors. He wore a suit that he reserved for Sundays and preached like he was talking to you over a cup of coffee. He was indeed, my kind of preacher. We enjoyed many years at that small church where I learned that preachers are just people. Maybe even the big-haired preachers are regular folks, although I don't know how they could ever wear an official little league hat.

Del's low-key style of ministry rapidly pulled in young families from the neighborhood. He was eventually sent to build up another struggling church so we lost contact except for Christmas cards.

I last saw Del on TV. He was still a competitor. I was watching a Seattle Mariners game at the old King Dome. A fan climbed out of the third base stands and argued with the umpire. Could it be? Yup. A phone call the next day from a friend confirmed it. The fan was Del. By then he was the pastor of a very big church, but without the hair.

The only thing that exceeded Del's passion for baseball was recruiting people to God. Del is now coaching on the Big Diamond in the sky. He was the kind of guy you wanted in the coach's box so I'm sure it will be no surprise to the angels if he stomps on his halo a time or two.

Coaching

The sign was of the usual homemade variety announcing a grand event at the local grade school: Little League Sign Ups, Wed. Night at 7:00 pm. It was already Wednesday night and just after seven so I pulled in to see what was going on.

"Do you have a son you'd like to sign up?" asked John Barnette.

"No, but I thought I might like to coach a team," I said.

" Ever coached before?" Barnette asked.

"Not exactly, but I played when I was a kid and my dad coached us so I think I could do a good job," I said.

"The Major and Minor league teams already have their coaches and we like to start our new coaches in the Farm league, with the eight to nine year olds," he said.

Barnette's tone told me that this was one of those highly competitive leagues that I had heard so much about, long before people were criticizing "soccer moms."

"If you do a good job there, then maybe you can get one of the Major teams," he said with casual indifference.

"Okay, do you have a Farm team that needs a coach?" I asked thinking maybe these guys needed a lesson or two in coaching manners.

"Yes, you can be the manager of the West Portland Lumber team." Then Barnette revealed the inner-workings of how teams win championships. "They play ten games and if you have a coach who has a son we can put him on your team and if he has a brother he can also be on your team."

"I don't know anybody in the league we've only been here a few months, but this sounds like a good place to start," I said.

Harking back to my own days of youth baseball, I knew this would be fun for our little family. I signed up and went home where Ardi waited with dinner and Robb, our four month old son. That was the start of nearly 30 years of coaching kids. Colossal!

***

Everything I learned about sports I learned from other coaches. There are a few basics that every coach teaches: 1. A positive attitude is a must. 2. Give 100% all of the time. 3. Team work comes first. These 3 principles apply to nearly every career that comes to mind. Establishing these fundamentals early in kids can go a long way toward influencing their choices in later years.

These few simple tenants are the big picture. Winning coaches get right down to the nitty-gritty of getting the most out of each player. One year I was coaching my youngest son Randall back in the farm league, while our second son, Ryan was playing on a local high school summer team. Ryan's coach had a history of winning while letting his players enjoy the game. One of his confidence building techniques was exceptional. I immediately stole/borrowed/made it my own.

As the high school game unfolded it became a pitcher's duel. The other team in the field was holding a one run lead in the bottom of the last inning. Our team had gotten the third, fourth and fifth batters on to load the bases. The sixth and seventh batter struck out and now the number eight batter was up. Since it was in the late innings he was one of the kids who rode the pines and was probably the eleventh or twelfth best hitter on the team.

"Look at this!" The coach shouts from the third base coach's box while doing a Michael Jackson, Moon-Walk. "We've got the right guy at the right time, just what we want!" That kid's chest puffed out, he flexed his jaw muscles, dug in his heels and hit it through the hole for a game winning single.

Would he have gotten a hit without the coach's flamboyant antics? Who knows, but the coach only used that technique with the players at the bottom of his order. As often as not, they came through. What did he have to lose?

The next Saturday Randall's farm team was playing its last game. I was only the assistant, to the assistant coach because I wanted to watch the games of our other kids and Randall was not an athlete like our other children. Sports came hard for him. He was severely dyslexic which means he wrote upside down and backwards. I have no idea how he must have seen a pitched ball. In soccer that year he had trouble figuring out which foot to use to kick the ball. He had yet to get a hit the entire season and he came up to bat in the bottom of the last inning with the bases loaded and we were down by three.

Using what I had learned from the game the night before, I went into my own rather ostentatious act.

"Holy smokes, lookie here!" I shouted while pumping my fist in the air and doing my own version of the Moon-Walk in the coach's box. (If you're not going to have fun, why do it?) "We've got the right guy up at the right time!"

The fans of both sides chuckled, as Randall stepped in with his usual determination and took a mighty swing. "Strike one," said the umpire as I Moon-Walked again and said, "Wasn't your pitch big guy."

The wind up, the pitch, and another mighty swing at a ball way outside. Randall always swung at the first three pitches, occasionally hitting a foul ball, but he didn't have a chance to put a bat on this ball. "Steeerrrrrike two," shouted the umpire.

"You didn't want that one anyway. Come on now, you're the right guy at the right time and it only takes one." That used up my entire bag of baseball clichés.

I was preparing for my usual run into the plate, getting all the kids around to give the winning team a rousing yell.

"Hey, batter, batter, swing" the fielders yelled. The pitcher delivered a heater right over the middle. Randall took a mighty cut and the metal bat went "plink," barely connecting with the ball. It landed fair.

"Fair ball, run like mad crazed dogs kids, everyone run!" I put my arm into the windmill motion just like my dad used to do when he was my coach.

We got a little help from the pitcher and a fortuitous bounce. Their kid on the mound would probably go on to pitch for the Yankees, he was that good. But as he ran to grab the spinning ball it took an odd bounce and he kicked it past the third baseman out into the field. Their fielder picked it up and threw a strike to second base, but Randall had rounded second and was heading to third and he knew what the windmill signal meant. At this level of play, two good throws would be impossible. As the ball sailed out of play he jumped on home plate to finish off his only hit and score of the season with a game winning, grand-slam, home run.

"You were the right guy at the right time," one of the parents said patting him on the back. He was as proud as I was shocked. It was a great way to end the season.

Randall had been struggling in school. In those days there was no exact diagnosis for dyslexia. Sports were difficult, but he liked to be around the other kids and this was his Colossal day to be the star.

"Dad," Randall said carrying the gear to the car, "Why don't you be the manager next year, you wouldn't have to play me an awful lot and it's fun to have you on the sidelines."

"We'll see son, (choke, cough, sputter, and wipe the eyes.) "We'll see."

***

Ah Hah!

When you leave your home vacant for most of the summer it becomes easy prey for burglars. We had nothing of real value, we took the usual security precautions, but as we left to spend that first summer at Camp Easter Seal there was a nagging feeling that something would happen.

Closing up Camp Easter Seal for the summer was work, with a capital "W." The camp was perched atop a 100 foot high isthmus that sloped into Ten Mile Lake creating one of the lake's many fingers and backwaters. The charm of the camp was its isolation. It could only be reached by a long boat ride. On the other hand, loading sixty handicapped campers in wheelchairs, their luggage, and an assortment of appliances into our two speedboats for the trip down the lake was a bone-tiring exercise. Our job wasn't done until every camper was loaded into a car or in some cases, hoisted onto a Greyhound Bus for their trip home.

With the last wave goodbye to campers and about 30 staff members, Ardi and I loaded up one of the boats with a summers worth of our clothes and all the paraphernalia that goes with an eight month old baby. The camp caretaker, V. W. Hankins, "Hank" to all who knew him, took us down to the dock where our '69, no frills, Chevy Impala awaited our arrival. It was always a struggle not to fall asleep during the four and a half hour trip to our new home in SW Portland. (It was usually a bit longer because it was hard to pass up a burger and milkshake at "Arlene's" in Elkton. Never met anyone who traveled through that part of Oregon who didn't avail themselves to this scrumptious diner with oiled wood floors pocked from the "calk boots" of many generations of loggers.)

The late August weather had me dripping in sweat as I dragged the baby's crib, along with tons of clothing into our brand new house on Portland's SW Vesta Street. Ardi put the baby in the crib and I threw open the windows. Not a leaf stirred on our wooded lot. It was so hot even the mosquitoes refused to fly. Out of Marine Corps habit, I did a perimeter check for any invaders. None found, I hopped into a lukewarm shower, dried off and slipped between the sheets of our new king-sized bed in my altogether. Exhaustion trumped heat. I was slumbering next to Ardi in no time.

Small, muffled noises in the entry had me instantly awake. Eighteen months earlier I had been sleeping in the sweltering heat of Vietnam. My "fight or flight" instincts still operated on high alert. These burglars were no match for a battle hardened war veteran. I would take no prisoners. My Marine Corps officer's sword had been placed under our bed. We weren't quite sure how to store it so it rested atop some still-to-be-hung pictures. It made no sound as I slipped it out of its metal scabbard. The element of surprise, essential in any battle, would be mine. The adrenalin rush was familiar and welcome. Wily, I slithered on my belly.

The Marine officer's sword is made for decoration, not combat, but it was relatively sharp. Combined with a strong grip, and unbridled fury for the protection of my family it would slice these intruders into fish bait for camp. Any weapon is only as good as the person wielding it. I would wield it wildly.

From the front door the hall was "L" shaped, with the small part of it ending in our bedroom. The hall light had a flip switch at both ends of the "L." Stealthily I got to my knees. For once they didn't crack as I arose. Camp was fun and games. This would be serious bloodshed.

In one motion I flipped the switch, raised my sword for a death dealing blow, jumped right at the burglars in a spread legged, Samurai position and shouted "Ah Hah!"

"Ah Hah yourself" said Uncle Clyde. "It's nice to see you" said Aunty Midge.

"oooohhhhhhkkkkayyyyy," I said, as casually as one can while standing like a nude ninja warrior while holding a sword above one's head. Realizing my shortcomings, I jumped back behind the L of the hallway and nonchalantly said "You kids make yourselves comfortable in the guest room and we'll see you in the morning." I put on the bottoms of my jammies and slipped back between the sheets. Ardi and Robb had slept like babies through the entire adventure.

During the bustle of camp life, it had slipped my mind that Ardi had given Aunt Midge and Uncle Clyde Dickey a key to our house so they could stop over on their way to California from their farm in Acme, Washington (two hours north of Seattle.)

All through breakfast Ardi still had no clue of the previous night's hubbub until I interrupted the rather stilted, awkward conversation about the weather, how's everybody doing, and etc., and asked Midge, a matronly, hardworking, and old fashioned farm gal, what she meant by "It's nice to see you?" Midge turned dark crimson, covered her face with her hands and profusely apologized over and over for not ringing the doorbell. Clyde and I went into fits of laughter and he almost snorted his milk.

The Dickeys have been gone for many years. The sword hangs in our living room as a remnant of my military past, but to be honest, it gives me a chortle whenever I think of Aunty Midge turning beet red that morning at breakfast. As many times as I have told this story at family reunions, I have never been able to figure out, other than that I have no shame, why she was the one who felt embarrassed.

***

Guard This Please

During a writer's convention at Portland State, per usual, I wore my ostentatious, Tyrolean hat covered with pins from the countries I've visited. A big turkey feather is stuck in it for good measure. I love wearing it because it screams "I am a writer!"

Indigo Editing, a book publisher, was conducting a thirty six word writing contest. The piece had to contain the word prompt "Savannah." I had retired to the student union mezzanine for its availability of comfy tables and chairs. While in my own world trying to coax the muses to bless me with three dozen words, a Vietnamese, student sat in a chair in close proximity. He takes out his iMac and begins pecking away. He says "Sir, would you mind watching my computer while I use the men's room."

"Be glad to" I say.

Shortly after he leaves a Vietnamese gal comes over and takes his seat. She says "This belongs to my friend and he asked me to take care of it for him." She picks up the computer and boldly begins to walk off with it.

I'm not one to be taken advantage of quite so easily.

"Hold on," I shout gaining her attention along with about 15 other people in the cozy little study area. "I was asked to watch that for someone and that's what I'm going to do."

"I'm just going to wait for him down by the elevator," she said.

"I'll wait with you because wherever that computer goes, I'm going," I said.

The elevator doors open and we start to get on. At that point another student peaks around the corner behind us with a video camera and says "Thanks for being a part of our experiment." And everybody has a good laugh.

As I return to my seat everybody in the entire place is now smiling, openly laughing, and clapping. As the Vietnamese kids leave, a member of the instant audience says "You know you should never mess with a guy with a feather in his hat." (he didn't even say, old guy with a..."

I boldly put on what my kids call "My old man hat" waved goodbye and walked confidently to turn in my story of thirty six words titled *Savannah*.

The closeness of tanned skin holding the scent of coconut oil ignited our starving young passions. A balmy night and a warm Georgia breeze blessed the joining. We smile when asked "Why is her name Savannah?"

My ditty tied for first place. It was a Colossal day!

***

The Birds and The Bees

Yup, I'm "old school." In our family we have a firm division of labor. I do the *manly* chores of mowing the lawn, emptying the garbage, and driving on long trips. I never ask for permission to go quaff a pint with the boys as long as I have finished my vacuuming.

It was therefore, always understood that Ardi would have "That Talk" about that four letter word, SEX with our children. It was the motherly thing to do. My job was to teach them to hit the ball, shoot hoops, and ride bikes.

The Colossal Life of Mr. Average

The manly role ended one spring day when there were two robins on our freshly mown lawn just outside the kitchen window. They were doing what birds do in the spring. You know, hopping, bumping, flapping their wings, in a goofy manner and more or less, acting…distressed. Our bird feeders attracted lots of our feathered friends and the kids knew the names of the common avian

With gleeful cries and beaming smiles the three boys rushed into the house pointing at the cavorting pair and gushed "Dad, what are the robins doing? Are they fighting? Maybe they're dancing?"

Terror struck my heart. It would be up to me to have "That Talk." It was the most teachable of moments that a father could have with his sons. "Go ask your Mom" quickly entered my mind. They were used to that response. It was better than "Get away from that window and go play in your rooms." There was no escape I would have to bite the bullet and teach my sons the facts of life. Beads of sweat formed on my forehead. I turned off the vacuum.

"Okay, it's time you kids learned about the birds and the bees. You remember those little blue eggshells we found last summer? Well, they were left when the baby robins hatched and every spring the momma and poppa robin come together and…"

"Oh that's what they're doing. We know all about that stuff Dad," the kids said.

I continued with my awkward heart-to-heart, "Now men and women like your mom and dad…"

"We know Dad! They teach us that in Health Class. You don't need to tell us anymore," the older boys, insisted. "Ya dad, we learn it in school" the kindergartner added as they headed out the door causing the robins to seek a more secluded venue.

Apparently we had smart kids who listened in school. My "Talk" was done, not as excruciating as I had expected, quite detailed, and nicely handled, if I do say so myself.

The deep thinker of the family, Randall, returned with a questioning look. Maybe my job wasn't finished.

"What's up son?" I asked.

"Dad, I know a lot about the birds...but I don't anything about the bees," he said with his head cocked in a questioning manner.

Where had I gone wrong? It was pointless to confuse him with something he would be learning in middle-school anyway so I said, "After I put in this load of wash, I'll get a Mason jar and we'll go catch a couple of bees like your old dad used to do. You can study them for yourself."

Like most fathers, I have no idea where my boys learned the facts of life. Probably the "old school" method, in the boys locker room??

***

A version of this story appeared in the "Everybody Has a Story section of The Columbian newspaper. The Editor said it was the "gooniest" story he had ever received. I think that is a compliment? My friend, Jack wrote a song about it and played it at a ukulele workshop. To view, simply Google Jack Norby Nacho.

Poetry Night

In the local scandal sheet I found an announcement for "Poetry Night" to be held at El Presidente, a well-known Mexican restaurant here in The Couve. The event would be hosted by Christopher Luna, the Clark County, Poet Laureate. To expand my knowledge of writing genres I decided to attend. It was my intention to be the proverbial "Fly on the wall" and absorb writing tips from a group of people (Poets) who, by definition, are of a creative bent.

The Poet Laureate gave us an introduction to *Haiku*. It is a Japanese form of poetry composed traditionally of lines with only 5, 7, and 5 syllable schemes in each line and usually about nature or love. Here's an example

A single poppy – 5 syllables

Blowing in a field of wheat – 7 syllables

Your face in a crowd – 5 syllables

There are no rules to Haiku. Mr. Luna assigns the group of about fifteen people the challenge of creating a Haiku with the line scheme of 4-3-4-3 syllables. Journals open, pens, and pencils etch beautiful words on handmade parchment and recycled paper in distinctive composition books. I am scribbling on the back of an extra placemat. Flies are not expected to write.

El Presidente serves free, oven-baked nachos with their own Vancouver-Famous salsa. I'm writing, munching, drinking beer and did I mention munching on the free stuff? I'm being as creative as I can be, but my mind is blank except for some silliness that ruins a good placemat.

As is customary at such events, participants are given the opportunity, if they wish, to stand and read their creation. It's strictly voluntary so I continue drinking and munching and enjoy listening to short, but exquisite, Haiku poems about nature and love. In a few cases, about the nature of love.

Every single person delivers their Haiku—except, The Fly. All eyes turn towards me. I politely decline and offer a few lame excuses. They insist…I have no shame so I explain that "I like my poems to rhyme and my method of writing is to just start writing and something will come to me, but tonight, it didn't. I did stick to the 4-3-4-3 syllable scheme, but I added some actions to my poem which makes it kind of fun and Haiku seems to have no rules."

The group is quiet. Blank stares await my genius. I turn over the placemat. I know my poem. I made it easy to remember. It's 14 syllables, with actions. I begin the Haiku of a lifetime.

Nachos, Nachos – 4 syllables

Clap, Clap, Clap – 3 syllables
(*I clap as I say Clap*)

Nachos, Nachos – 4 syllables

In my lap – 3 syllables

There arose one of those awkward silences when people don't know whether to laugh or cry. Some are embarrassed for me. I easily get over it. A little water had taken care of the salsa blotch on my new slacks. My confidence grew. Then I have the group recite and clap along with me. People are belly-laughing. I think that's original to poetry readings.

My kids and grandkids get a kick out of my "Nachos" poem. That's all that matters.

To those who think my ditty is less than genius, "Well, Haiku To You Too."

Chapter 4

Old Stories

The BA

When a male freshman first steps onto a college campus his entire body conspires against him. His pituitary gland, medulla oblongata, frontal lobes, and testes transform him into a Dolt; a foolish person who enjoys grown up freedoms while ignoring adult responsibilities. Released from the teenage annoyance of hovering parents he searches for sex and booze like an Aardvark diving into an anthill. Male freshmen, desperate to achieve collegiate maturity regress to juvenile twits.

A brain, who needs it? Raging hormones and testosterone levels that are running rampant are his conscience. In the first three weeks of class he will have had some awkward sex that gets him to first base. An all-night beer session will lead to a pseudo-intellectual discussion about religion causing him to skip an early morning class.

During the sixties this unbridled exuberance led to Streaking, Goldfish Swallowing, Phone Booth Body-Stuffing, and other random acts of goofiness. Linfield College embraced this national zaniness by revering the Moon. Not the celestial body that waxes and wanes, but the dropping of ones pants, bending over and exposing one's bare derriere. The exposed hams became a synonym for a Moon and achieved the acronym known as a BA.

Dolt behavior took on artistic forms of display. The BA mashed against a car window became a Pressed Ham. You got Faced when a BA was planted on your face while taking a nap. The Double Inverted BA was achieved by two people interlocking elbows back to back. One bends over while the other gymnastically rests on the back of his partner with his bare butt and legs up in the air simultaneously delivering two BAs.

In one grand display of rear-ends on a spring evening in 1962 the practice came to an ignoble end. The obscene, scene took place between the five men's dorms which were situated on the far side of the campus. Four of them faced each other across a quad in north and south positions. The fifth was on the east side creating the cross piece of a U tipped on its side with the open part facing west.

Memorial Hall, the east dorm, was actually built into the football stadium. The ceilings in most rooms looked like upside downs stairs because of the stadium's bleacher seating. Football players loved this ancient dorm.

The stereotype of knuckle dragging, sloped headed, football players fit many of the Memorial residents. They were intelligent, academically competent, but lacked any social graces. Giving BA's was as natural to them as grunting and groaning in the weight room. It was almost predictable that they would bring BAs to a crescendo of finality.

On a spring night just before dark I heard garbage can lids banging together.

"What's going on?" I asked my roommate.

"I dunno," Wayne Carlson said. "It looks like the guys in Memorial are up to something again."

"If it's water balloons I'm not getting into it. They got licked in the last fight, but they retaliated with fire hoses on the guys in Anderson Hall. They flooded their rooms in the middle of the night."

The windows of the north and south dorms were crowded with students cheering like a village just liberated in WWII. A group of about twenty football players were marching between them in single file. The lids clanged together like symbols keeping a crisp military cadence. Their leader wore a Nazi German helmet and wielded a toilet plunger like a drum major's scepter. In a drill sergeant's voice he called out, "Your left, your left, your left right left." When they reached the middle of the Quad they stopped and stood at attention. "Ones left and twos right," he shouted. Half of the players turned to face north, and half faced south, creating a line with every other person facing a different dorm. The next command was, "Drop Trou." They all pulled down their pants. "Present BA," and they all dutifully bent over and BA'd the dorms. Another command was barked and they partnered up, hooked elbows and gave the double inverted BA. "Up trou, right face, forward march," the leader ordered. They marched off to the clanging of the lids and the hoots, howls, and whistles from the violated dorms.

It was an all-male cast performing for an all-male audience, with the exception of the dorm mothers, who did not shock easily at a little nudity. It was gross, not pornographic, but like art, porno is in the eye of the beholder.

"Linfield is a Christian school supported by Baptist congregations all around the country. A high standard of behavior is required of all students. It violates all public decency," Dennis Schweitzer said mimicking Doctor Boling as he laughingly told us what the Dean had said.

The laughing ended the next day when they were all suspended for two semesters. It seemed severe for a little premeditated silliness that visits all college campuses in the spring. The immediate consequences meant that Dennis could not play baseball or football in the calendar year of 1962. On top of that, he had to tell his parents that he was suspended for wagging his bare rump at a bunch of men. But, no one could suspect that over thirty years later this misadventure would look like it was choreographed by Divine Intervention.

In 1963, Dennis, was the only student who returned from the suspension. As he resumed his studies and returned to playing baseball and football he was tagged Dirty Denny.

In the fall of 1965 Dirty was voted a team captain of the football team. He was instrumental in leading the team to the championship game of the National Association of Intercollegiate Athletics. Linfield got crushed in that game, but Dirty garnered NAIA, All-American honors. In the spring of 1966, he played baseball as a fifth year senior. He was a first baseman, pitcher and a solid hitter. That season the baseball team went on to win Linfield's first National Championship in any sport.

When he graduated in June, the BA incident was all but forgotten. He now had some impressive credentials for starting his life as a high school football coach. It would be a good story if it just ended right here. But the full ramifications would lay dormant for over three decades.

Duper (Super Duper) was another fifth year senior playing on that baseball team. After retiring in 1999 from a successful thirty three year teaching and coaching career, he had a complete kidney failure. He went through the stages of dialysis and eventually needed a kidney transplant. Duper's son was a perfect match for the kidney but he would not accept his son's offer because it would have disqualified him from becoming an airline pilot. Duper's other name is Stubborn, but he scored a lot of points with his friends for not letting his son give up on his dream.

In the year 2000 the 1966 NAIA National Championship Baseball Team was inducted into the Linfield College Hall of Fame. During the banquet the seating arrangements placed Dirty and Duper side by side. They had not seen each other for over thirty years. They caught up on each other's lives and talked like they were still sitting in the dugout. Good friends do that.

During the nineties Dirty became a Christian. Everyone he met he politely asked them not to call him Dirty Denny because he was a totally different person. He said that he never attended any of the college functions because he was too embarrassed about his early years and didn't want people to treat him like the Dirty Dennis of old. Nobody did.

Duper told him about needing a kidney, "Given the progression of the disease, time's not on my side," he added.

"I'll give you a kidney," Dennis said.

"You don't understand Denny, a match from somebody off the street is nearly impossible."

"But it is possible," Dennis said.

In the next few weeks when Dennis prayed for Duper he heard an inner voice asking, "Why not you?" He talked it over with his family and they agreed he should get tested.

"Duper, God called me to do this. He blessed me with a matching kidney," Dennis said over the phone like an excited father telling about a newborn baby.

Duper was dumbfounded but he was too sick to argue. Within weeks the two, sixty year old men shared one pair of kidneys. As of this writing Duper will make his tenth trip to Korea as a Fulbright Scholar and Dennis continues to be as healthy as ever.

"Got Religion?" The odds for a happy ending to this story are long enough to turn a felonious reprobate into a Franciscan Monk. Any thought that a school suspension for a BA could have a positive outcome assaults one's good taste and challenges all common sense. The chances of Dennis playing on a national championship team for a tiny school were astronomical. A banquet that united two players who have not seen each other for thirty four years is extraordinarily fortuitous. The odds of a kidney match from a non-relative are a **million to one**. The real grabber, Dirty Dennis turned his life completely around enough to even offer up a prayer asking for a statistical anomaly to extend the life of a friend.

"God works in strange ways," is a phrase we've all heard devout people say when they have no answers. I have to agree with them, but I want to add that God must have a sense of humor. God must have quietly chortled when He said to Himself "I think I'll start this miracle off with a BA. The world needs to know that some people who seem to be the worst, turn out to be the best."

(After 13 years with the new kidney, Dale Hayward passed away, but Denny's Colossal gift gave all of us more fun years with Duper.)

***

The Lesson

This story is from a day when I was student teaching a lesson on creative writing to eighth graders. This little gal was a bit of a handful, but this assignment was to write a first sentence that would grab the reader. She knocked it out of the park!

"Judy had suffered abuse by her father, was disgraced by teen pregnancy, and at fourteen she was saddled with motherhood."

After she shared her work, the class went quiet and so did I. It took me a few seconds to comprehend the depth of the sentence the eighth grader had just read.

She was the last reader. Just before the bell rang I managed to say "Paige, that's a great name for a writer and you've just hooked all of us. I hope you'll finish your story."

***

This story was told to me many years ago. I wrote it soon afterward. While doing a little research for this epistle, I have discovered that after years of retelling a favorite tale, even the originator changes what is first described as the "Gospel Truth." It's how the aging mind works. It is a good thing. I hereby swear that the main elements of the following saga are mostly true.

Blue Moon

Small college athletes feel the "Thrill of victory and Agony of Defeat," with the same intensity as their big school and professional sports counterparts. They are a few sizes smaller and a step or two slower, but when the endorphins kick in after a win they get the same ecstatic experience as the Super Bowl champs. Conversely, after a tough loss, an imbalance of serotonin creates a depression that leaves them feeling lower than whale manure in the Mariana Trench.

Keep in all of the emotions, but take out the money, the scholarships, any likelihood of playing professionally, and you are down to the basics of what sports should be; for the love of the game. That's NCAA, Division III sports. In our day it was the National Association of Intercollegiate Athletics.

If you were part of an athletic team at Linfield College, student population of a little over 1000, in the sixties, the experience has lasted a lifetime. The coaches instilled in players a loyalty to their teams and to each other. The result has been lasting friendships, business partnerships, coaching relationships, and beach houses purchased together by teammates. The Linfield colors of cardinal and purple are entwined together in a thread that has been stitched into the life fabric of nearly every athlete of our era.

The charm of a small school was that you got to know the players in other sports. I got to know Wayne Peterson because he worked on the chain crew during football games. I swept the gym floor during the basketball season where he was an all-star player. Wayne had the whole package; talent and commitment. He worked hard at the grades and at his sport. He was the type of player that deflected his personal accolades to the credit of his teammates. When asked by a reporter about his; off the dribble, twisting, jumping, thirty foot, buzzer-beating, swishing shot to win a game, he made it sound like the pass from his team mate was already going in the hoop and all he did was give it a little boost. "Pete" as we called him, was more than the ordinary team captain. He was a mother hen and made sure that all the players worked out hard during the off season and did his best to keep them from running afoul of training rules at the local watering hole, "The Blue Moon."

Every college had one, but by any other name, it's still "The Moon," a cheap beer pub where players and students met in the off season to have a little fun off the field or court. The conversation never strayed too far from sports, school, and girls. That's the college version of "Mother, God, and Apple Pie." I don't remember Pete ever imbibing at The Moon, but I can assure you, he would never let anybody have more than a couple of beers or sully the reputation of a promiscuous coed. He would remind everyone to, "Do The Right Thing." He took his religion of "The Team" into life like Billy Graham took the Gospel to the masses. Pete "Walked the Talk," as the saying goes.

Forty years later The Blue Moon is still our Mecca. We make the pilgrimage after each football game. The odor of stale beer, cigarettes and old French fries with fury stuff on them engulfs your senses like the muggy heat of a Chicago summer clings to your body. One whiff and we salivate like Pavlov's dogs for bargain beer and a conversation which we know will make us young for a few hours. It's a reality-based, time warp. We are still ordering beer from the same barmaid that tended our table when we were in school. Back in the day, we thought she was old, but Doris couldn't have been much over thirty. The owner hasn't aged one wrinkle and the locals on the bar stools look like the same red faced, beer drinkers from four decades ago. I suspect it's the same faces, but different people. The men's room still has the customary bucket of ice in the tall, old-fashioned, urinal. There is no gas trap in the plumbing so the ice cools the air in the sewer pipe and prevents the fumes from migrating back out the urinal filter. I wondered how many buckets of ice had been used over forty years and was the green plastic bucket ever used for anything else?

At a thirty year-or-so reunion, Don Wilson, AKA "Weasel," got up to visit the men's comfort station. Out of the blue I said "Weasel, I'll bet you twenty bucks there's ice in the urinal." He took the bet, announcing it was some sort of "Fergy insanity." Upon his return he sheepishly handed me a Jackson, with his distinct, little boy, caught with a hand in the cookie jar, grin. I told him the story of the ice. We all laughed and enjoyed a pitcher of beer purchased with his money. Don left us a while back, but that look on his face is still with me.

The time capsule was complete with yellow and orange cone shaped lights dangling from the ceiling providing just enough light to barely read the menu. The dark brown, overstuffed, vinyl, half circle booths could seat about six. With some chairs we could get about eight people comfortably around the booth. After a few beers the games of our youth are replayed over and over again. It's uncanny how game scores and small details can be remembered when the gentlemen telling them can't remember where they have parked their cars. Our college exploits have become larger, more daring, and now approach epic proportions. "The older we get, the better we were." It's fun. It's like the war stories told at the meetings of the Veterans of Foreign Wars, partially true.

Some of the fun now comes from more recent stories about generational gaffs that come with age. Jack Forde, a teammate of Pete's, regaled us with a beauty after a game several years ago.

"Do you guys remember Tom Leatherwood?" Jack asked the gathering.

"You mean the basketball player, he rode the bench mostly, didn't he?" Asked one of the Ol' Wildcats.

"Ya, that's the guy. He wasn't a starter, but he was a hard worker and lot of fun on the road. He was one of Coach Wilson's favorites because of his work ethic," Jack said.

"What about him, he win the lottery, or something?" Asked an imbiber, impatiently waiting for Jack to commence his saga.

"Well several years ago his name was in the obituaries. You remember Rick Pullen, the Sports Information guy for the school when we were here? Well, he worked for the Oregonian and an obituary just happened to land on his desk before it went to print. He saw Leatherwood's name. The age of the guy was just right, and Pullen knew he had he a girlfriend named Theresa so he's positive it's our Tom Leatherwood. He thinks it's not much of an obituary because it's just his name and the usual info about his family. So Pullen dresses it up and adds all the stuff about Tom playing basketball and being an assistant coach at Linfield. Then he gives the details about the funeral service." Jack was warming to his subject.

"I read it, and thought it was pretty well done," said a voice in the booth.

"So did I," Jack says. "But get this, I get a call the same night that I read the obit and a voice says, 'The rumors of my demise have been greatly exaggerated, this is Leatherwood.' Of course I'm shocked, but I said you sound an awful lot like Mark Twain. How come you're not dead like you're supposed to be?" Jack then gave us his inimitable, uninhibited laugh.

When Jack lets out one of his patented, whoops you can't keep from laughing with him. We're all guffawing, half at how he's telling the story, and half at the predicament of getting a call from a dead guy. The beer was working its magic. It felt exactly like forty years ago when we'd finished our last finals and wandered into the Moon like a herd of parched Gnus at an oasis on the Serengeti. We were having fun.

"Then Leatherwood tells me all about what Pullen did so I told him that a bunch of us had been planning to go to his funeral on Saturday so he better get the word out to the team and I told him I'd call some of the guys for him. It was late on a Friday night and Wayne Peterson wasn't home and never got called and you all know Pete, he would be there for sure," Jack said.

Indeed, we know Pete. He's still the responsible row-monitor that he was in the third grade. He received a lot of well-deserved, local press early in his coaching career for taking a baseball team with only eleven players and winning the Oregon State High School Championship. The quote in the paper was true to his character, "I was blessed with a lot of talent so it was easy." We knew better. It was his ability to instill his love of sports, competitiveness, and work ethic into the kids. Pete will forever be a mother hen.

Naturally he quickly moved up to athletic director and onto becoming a principal. Always button down, sharp dresser, I never heard him swear, and if he cut himself shaving, he'd bleed cardinal and purple. Therefore, it was expected of him to attend the funeral and send flowers for the service.

"Pete had never met Tom's wife so at the service he introduces himself to the family and extends his condolences, but Pete was really steamed at his old team mates for not showing up. They had let a teammate down by not going to his funeral and he would let those 'son-of-a-bucks' know it," Jack said.

Jack imitates Pete's voice at the funeral in what had to be an interesting encounter, "I'm terribly sorry for your loss Mrs. Leatherwood, he was such a great person to have on the team. He was one of Coach Wilson's favorite players because he worked so hard. All the time Mrs. Leatherwood had to be thinking, 'Who in the world is this guy, did he come for the food at the wake?"

"It gets even better," Jack says with a gleam in his eye. "Leatherwood calls Pete that night after the funeral and says, 'Hey Pete this is Tom Leatherwood' and before he can say anything else Pete says, 'I don't know who you are buddy, but you've got a sick sense of humor and if you call here again I'll call the police,'" Jack said imitating the flat, terse principal tone that all of us could imagine coming from Pete.

"So Leatherwood thinks, 'Oh, Oh, I better not call him again, he's really ticked off.' He doesn't know what to do so he calls me and tells me what Pete said and that I'd better call him to give him the real scoop. Well, I saw an opportunity," Jack said, like it was the biggest real estate deal of a lifetime. We are bending over laughing. We knew a "Rascal" plan was about to emerge. "So everybody I talked with just decided to keep Pete in the dark about Leatherwood," Jack says chuckling as he talks.

It was inevitable that the team would have a reunion. Many years after the faux, funeral for Leatherwood the team met and Leatherwood shows up. As is customary at such gatherings, everyone tells what they have been doing for the last several years. Jack says, after we regained our composure, "Pete gets up and says 'I've been mad at you Sons-a-Bucks for ten years for missing the funeral, but it's nice to see Tom is still with us."

Jack's story, his enthusiasm for Pete's embarrassment, and his infectious, laughter had tears running down the cheeks of this Linfield-Forever-Wildcat, squad. Through the years we have laughed with, and at each other. Everyone has taken their turn in the barrel. It was nice to finally get Pete in the laughed at category.

We kept chortling to ourselves while filing out of the door we had flung open hundreds of times. Each one of us is thinking how we will give Pete the raspberry the next time we see him. That's what good friends do.

The apple I had purchased from a roadside vendor snapped in my mouth as I bit into it. It was as crisp as the late fall air that pinched my nose and cheeks. Life has been apple sweet. I wondered, "Will St. Peter let me slip a booth from the Moon through the Pearly Gates so my friends will know where to find me?"

The following obituary was sent to me by Jack Forde. The wording is exactly as printed in the *Oregonian*.

Ex-Linfield player, coach dead at 29

Requiem Mass for Tom Leatherwood, a former basketball player and assistant coach at Linfield College will be at 10 a.m. Monday in Holy Trinity Catholic Church. Burial wil be in Mt. Calvary Cemetery.

Mr. Leatherwood, who was 29, lost control of his bicycle Thursday on Cornelius Pass Road north of Cornell Road and was hit by a truck after falling into the road. He died later in a Portland hospital.

He played for Linfield in 1963-1967 and was an assistant basketball coach during the 1968-1969 season. He later coached at Yamhill-Carlton High School.

Mr. Leatherwood was born in Alameda, Calif., but lived most of his life in Oregon and resided in the Aloha area for the past 2 years. He was employed by Tektronics, Inc. Survivors include his wife, Theresa; son Aaron; parents, Mr. and Mrs. Chester Leatherwood of Eugene; brother, Paul of Anchorage, Alaska; two sisters, Jeannette Groesz of Eugene and Patrice Lussier of Cloverdale; and grandmother, Mrs. Joseph Gendron of Berkeley, Calif.

Note: A few years ago I ran into Pete at an Easter church service. He and his wife, (the former Susie Helser and daughter of Pete's baseball coach, Roy Helser,) were serving coffee after the program. We began chatting about the old days and what we are doing in retirement. As we were leaving I asked Pete, "How'd you finally find out Leatherwood was still amongst the living?" He gave me sheepish grin and said "I'm not telling ya, it's too embarrassing." Colossal!

***

Ode to a Ceramic Fern

by Bob Ferguson

    I posit that only art which plucks the heart strings or moves one to belly-busting laughter is worthy of being acquired. Anything else is merely—decoration. With that as our requisite, we have collected art through the years that has a family story. There is Aunty Dirlam's first ever, amazingly beautiful water color done at age ninety. We are left to wonder what might have been. Through the confines of a train we oohed and aahed at a landscape with a centuries old farm house nestled in the Austrian Alps. The next day we were astonished to see that exact landscape just being hung in a gallery by the artist. We had to have it. And on our mantle rests a foot high, bronze colored, sculpture titled *Froggin'*. It has taken nearly half a century for it to be created.

    The story of Froggin' begins with my first project for a college art class in the early sixties. It was an 8" x 11" piece of work depicting various geometric shapes in assorted shades of blue. The professor extolled the virtues of the creations displayed by my fellow art students, but he was flummoxed when he came to my blue contribution and said "Well…uh…it's…a…well… it's nothing… but blue Scribbling." The students were kind enough not to laugh out loud and I didn't have to claim the anonymously submitted "scribbling" until after class. It would have gone unnoticed—except for Dave Finster, my incorrigible roommate. He knew it was my handiwork. To my severe indignity, he told everyone on campus about my "Blue Scribbling." Luckily I am blessed with the skin of an armadillo because, for the rest of my college days, whenever Finster, AKA "Fin," and I quaffed adult beverages, my artwork provided large quantities of laughter.

For years I shifted my "Blue Scribbling," around the garage. Each move gave me a warm chuckle. Then one day I realized that my children's kindergarten, finger paintings were better than my college artwork. My "Blue Scribbling" was then relegated to the dumpster. (As I write this document I rue that day. It would be a hilarious testament to a fun story that is over a half-century old.)

Fin was waiting just outside baggage claim at PDX. Ardi and I were picking him up the day before the '65 Champion Bowl football team was to be inducted into Linfield's Athletic Hall of Fame. He greeted me with a shout from the past "Hey, Blue Scribbler!" In ten seconds we had picked up in mid-sentence a conversation that began back in our basement apartment when we were nineteen-year-old college students.

We caught up on the last forty five years during the short ride to McMinnville. At noon we were meeting other teammates at the hotel. We all realized that outside of McMinnville, our Hall of Fame honor is small potatoes, but to the forty three players who attended, it was a tribute of a lifetime. We would cherish, what we knew that for some, would be our last time together.

By noon the hotel hospitality room was filled with as much testosterone as a large group of guys on Medicare could muster. The beer and stories flowed. Fin recounted many times the "Blue Scribbling" story. The tales were outrageous, but guys swore on the lives of their ex-wives that every detail was true. Then Terry Durham, AKA "The Frog" took the floor. He's animated, eyes laughing, great voice inflection, he's a character as big in life as Shrek is on the silver screen. Instead of *Frog* his nickname should have been "Taxi." His ears stick out like the doors on a taxi cab.

"Boys," he says gaining our rapt attention for what we knew would be a fun story. "Remember that drill where the defensive man lays on his back between two blocking bags and the offensive back gets a ball and tries to run between the bags without getting tackled?" He says while looking around the room for an answer.

Frog sets the stage using two beer cans for the upright blocking dummies. "That's the Oklahoma drill," someone remembers.

"Well, I sneak into the drill," Frog says. He uses a cube of cheddar cheese like a Monopoly piece as himself on one side of the beer cans. "Quarterbacks aren't supposed to be in tackling drills, but I get in it anyway and I have to go against The Fern," he says pointing at me using one of my Fern, Ferg, and Fergy nicknames. My Monopoly piece is a celery stick that he places on the other side of the beer cans.

"I get the ball and I get past him," the Frog says manipulating the cube of cheese between the beer cans and past the celery stick.

"Hold it right there, that's Horse Puckey! You were never fast enough to get past me," I say as I picked up his piece of cheese and ate it. Frog ignores me, grabs another piece of cheese and continues unabated.

"Then I feel these two big arms wrap around me and Fern slams me to the ground hurting me on purpose just because I'm CS, the Coach's Son, and I'm out for three games. That's a true story boys," Frog says raising his arms like exclamation points.

"True my derriere, if I had wanted to hurt you, you would have been out for the season. And, you were so painfully slow you should've been a lineman and I should've been the quarterback," I jibbed.

Frog adds "My dad was so mad at me he didn't speak to me for two weeks." We revered Coach Durham and we all knew that the toughest position on any team was that of the Coach's Son. The CS had to prove conclusively that he earned his position. The Frog did, but that's another story.

The Colossal stories continued into the wee hours. Nobody wanted this event to end, but it had to—if for no other reason than the local 7-Eleven stores had run out of beer.

The next morning some of the lads had to "Get the hair off the dog" before continuing with a pre-game, tail-gate party. The game was a good one, but it and even the induction ceremony became secondary to what was important, the gathering of stellar men for the last time.

Dave Finster had become an accomplished artist. He displays in studios in Oregon and Colorado. On the way back to the airport that Sunday, he asked me what he could do for me. I asked him to use his considerable talents to fashion something he remembers about the weekend. Several weeks later a package arrived at our home. After carefully unpacking it I am awed by Fin's artistic abilities.

Arising from a muddy gridiron is a massive figure with a transformer's leg of indestructible might. The other leg looks like it could have belonged to the legendary Bronko Nagurski and the torso is reminiscent of Jim Brown in its muscularity. The number 33 on the back is definitive proof that this colossus can be none other than—my-own-fine-self. Ruthlessly I am tackling a figure that looks somewhat like the frog you dissected in a high school biology class, complete with webbed feet wrapped around me in a splayed fashion. The number 15 on its back stamps the wilted figure as "The Frog." A deflated football rolls off my back as we clash in an earth shaking collision. The inscription reads "To The Fern 'Froggin.'" For some fun, Google: Froggin by Fin!-youtube.

The Goliaths of "Froggin" are forever locked in a struggle that can neither diminish nor gain in vigor. It is a portal into an event long past. The captured spirit will outlive the actors. Whenever I unveil "Froggin" amongst football friends, it starts the room giggling, then chortling, and grows into deep belly laughing. It is a welcome guest at all gatherings. It is my kind of art.

In the quiet of the family room I sit in my easy chair while Froggin' looks down at me from the mantle. I think back to that once-in-a-lifetime weekend and the countless laughs I've had with Fin. It is no coincidence that my author's business card is inscribed with… "Scribbler."

Chapter 5

Non-Creative Fiction

The following four fiction pieces, "My Summer of Blues," "Riff-Raff," "Occupy the Bacon," and "Thorsday Nights" were each written during one of the annual, 36 hour, "Sledgehammer Writing Contest." Riff-Raff won the "Reader's Choice Award" and I read it at the Portland, Wordstock Convention. There were 4 prompts that had to be found during a 2 hour scavenger hunt all around Portland. Then 34 hrs. of writing fun began! I wish I could remember what the prompts were, but as in all of my stories, the characters are derived from people I have actually met.

My Summer of Blues

Schazaaam! The sound was like a flashbulb going off inside of my head. My heart pounded and my palms were sweaty. I slammed on the brakes. The balmy August air mixed with a few brewskies already had me in a fog, but this marvelous jolt of music, was pouring out the door of the Mock Crest Tavern. It was too compelling to ignore.

The '97 Camry slipped into the first available parking space. I leaned against the car to catch my breath and collect my thoughts. My pulse raced, my senses were heightened, but I was still in control of my faculties. My feet started moving toward the exhilarating sound that had caused my end-of-life symptoms. Along with clouds of cigarette smoke, the sound wafted out into the night air under a faded neon sign. The greenish words "Mock Crest" were arched over "Tavern," which blinked erratically in pale pink.

The adrenaline rush made me feel like a kid of nineteen. I was compelled to find out what kind of sound could have penetrated my body deeper than an ex-ray. The two sided sandwich board announced music by "Johnny Ward and the Eagle Riding Pappas." It was about 9:30 on a Tuesday night. I had to see what kind of motorcycle gang had caused my near delirium.

The bar held a healthy dose of excitement. As I crossed the threshold I was greeted with the notes from a steel guitar, upright bass, harmonica, mandolin, the rat-a-tat-tat of a washboard percussionist. They were all fused with a sultry voice pounding out a song with the slight brag that "I picked Ol' Robin clean." It looked like a scene straight from the Mississippi Delta. The end of the song was greeted with a thunderous applause. The band leader declared a "Tip Jar" contest. "Put your name on a large bill and if it is picked out of the jar at closing time you win…..a great big thank you."

The music was only part of the aura. The humor of the band, the smoke curling up from ashtrays, and the surly language of the blue collar crowd intoxicated me. I was smitten.

I had been headed home after the monthly meeting of my writer's critique group. For the first time they had given me some positive feedback about my memoir, "Some Days Chicken, Some Days Feathers." I was ready for more excitement. The "Eagle Ridin' Pappas" filled that bill.

Johnny looked the part of a blues player. He wore a leather, newspaper boy hat, Hawaiian shirt, black shorts, and sandals, played the steel guitar while simultaneously blowing on a harmonica attached to a frame encircling his neck. In addition, he sang the male vocals, and slipped in a jug or kazoo with some of the songs.

Bill, the bass player, wore his hair in a luxurious gray pony tail that dangled past his waist. He played his huge "Dog House" bass while wearing a navy blue T-shirt advertising Budweiser, khaki cargo shorts and flip-flops. The picture of comfort.

While scrutinizing the band, I wormed my way to the back of the shoe-box shaped barroom that was crammed with people. One corner of the dimly lit bar looked like a tattoo convention for reprobates. Another cranny was filled with fresh faced kids out on a pub crawl before returning to the University of Portland. The chest high table with no chairs was surrounded by bearded men in baseball caps. They still wore the Carhartt pants they had worn to work on the docks earlier in the day.

The percussion section was Paul, another gentleman with a gray pony tail, albeit it thinner and shorter than Bill's. A wash board hung in front of his chest held by leather shoulder straps like a reverse backpack. He strummed it with thimbles on his fingers and occasionally, when the beat called for it, striking one of the "C" pitched cow bells or wooden blocks. Paul's attire consisted of a, red and white, plaid shirt, with long sleeves rolled up. It blended with his faded jeans held up by a big cowboy belt buckle. The ensemble was completed with red, PF Flyer sneakers.

In the back there was one available chair at a table where an elderly couple was seated. They looked like a small isle of conservatism in a rough sea of liberal sub-cultures. The gentleman was wearing tan pants, a pale blue polo shirt and white tennis shoes. The lady wore a scooped neck, purple blouse. Her collection was topped off by large purple ear rings. Students, dock workers, neighbors, and retirees, were mixed in a cauldron of music, food and good spirits. The bar was filled with a thick layer of cigarette smoke, but to me, it was a breath of fresh air.

The female lead for the Papas was Lauren, a consummate mandolin and guitar player. She was in her forties wearing a long flowered dress that reminded me of the hippy days. She is not only a mean picker on any stringed instrument, but sings with an evocative tone in a memorable voice.

Their appearance seemed one part stage persona and one part, whatever they had on when they rushed out the door to make the gig. It was unimportant. "The Eagle Ridin' Pappas" were all about their music. They made the old blues and folk greats their own. Their original songs were as timeless as a Muddy Waters classic.

As the waitress bobbed and weaved her way between the jostling bodies back to the bar I asked, "Do you really serve Pabst Blue Ribbon or is that just an old sign?"

"PBR is the most popular beer around here." She looked at me like I was from another planet and handed me a $2.50 pint of the golden elixir.

Pabst was the cheap beer that my father drank. I didn't know it was still brewed. It is a tribute to capitalism; make a good product, sell it cheap, and it will enjoy a long life.

Everybody shuffled their feet and bobbed their heads to the down beat. I did the same while holding my chilled pint of PBR. I soaked up the soulful music about "…losing my baby," "Working for the man," and "Trying to earn a dollar." The pounding rhythm invigorated the blood in my veins and made me young. The "Blues" is a music you feel.

As I became more intoxicated with the music, a thought occurred to me, "How had I lived 65 years and missed this superb music that was decades old?" It became painfully obvious to me. Imperceptibly, one day being less eventful than the previous, I had slipped into the mind-set of a sedentary, curmudgeon. This was my summons to wake up and "Catch the Blues!"

My burst of youthfulness was short-lived. My wrenched back complained and I needed a place to sit down. The empty chair at the table of the nattily dressed couple beckoned. The gentleman saw me gawking. "Have a seat, young fella" he said.

"Thank you. I'm Bob Ferguson, from Vancouver," I said.

"I'm Arnie Mills, and this is my wife, Velma." I shook Velma's hand and she said "It's nice to meet you."

The band took a break just as I sat down. "Do you live close by?" I asked.

"We used to live a few blocks down on the bluff, but now we live in a retirement home just around the corner" Arnie said.

Velma said nothing. She smiled at everybody who walked by. I wondered why the chair had been empty in such a crowded bar. Had their age made them irrelevant to the younger crowd? Did they have nothing to offer? Maybe they really wanted to be left alone and I had intruded.

A few cheap PBRs on top of the micro-brews I had down the street had my jaws flapping.

"Do you come here often?" I asked.

"Only when they start the music at eight. Much past that we get tuckered out," Arnie said, while Velma smiled in agreement.

Next to his pint of beer sat a black baseball cap emblazoned with "US Marines" arched over "WW II Veteran." Maybe the chair was empty because he was one of those guys who liked to sit and tell war stories. He was a Marine. I had no choice.

"Thank you for serving," I said, pointing to his cap. "Where did your travels take you?"

"I was in the third assault wave on Omaha Beach," he said. "From there we moved all over Europe until the war ended."

"What did you do in the Marines?" I was compelled to ask.

"I was a squad leader the whole time and we never did anything stupid," he said. "Only three guys out of our fifteen got wounded and none of us were killed."

"It's not every day that I get a chance to meet somebody that saw the invasion from the start to finish," I said.

The band returned and tuned up for their next set. The conversation ended. Bodies began to move and heads bobbed in what resembled a tribal dance to the rhythmic beat.

At Ten O'clock Arnie and Velma called it a night. I left an hour later and like Arnie, I dropped a few bucks in the tip jar and thanked the band for a spectacular evening.

The music still swirled in my head. I scanned the radio dial and found a blues station. I tapped the steering wheel in time with the music as I drove home to The Couve. The events, mixed with the booze were euphoric.

The next day I told my wife, Ardi about the critique group, but not about my foray into a blues bar. She wouldn't understand. We were in our mid-sixties and taverns had never been a part of our lives. Our kids were our lives. But now they were gone so what was the harm?

The first Tuesday of the next month, right after our critique group was over, I headed to the Mock Crest. Arnie and Velma were at the same small table. The bar was jam-packed, but the chair was still vacant. I didn't wait; "May I join you again?"

Velma shook my hand and said "It's nice to meet you."

"She's a little forgetful,' Arnie said, "but you don't throw away 58 years of marriage for a little inconvenience like that."

Velma smiled at Arnie and gave him the look that hooked him decades ago when he was a dashing young Marine.

I became a regular at "The Mock." My drink of choice was PBR because it was cheap enough that I could afford to buy Arnie an occasional round. Velma always greeted me with, "It's nice to meet you." Arnie and I chose the Marine Corps greeting of Semper Fi and swapped stories, but rarely about our war experiences.

The obituary of my new friend read:

> Arnold Mills, April 16, 1916 – November 10 2010, died peacefully in his sleep. He served with distinction in the U.S. Marine Corps and was awarded the Purple Heart and Silver Star for extreme heroism. He returned to his home town of Portland and became a machinist and worked in the Portland ship yards. He married Velma May Hinson, his high school sweetheart. She still lives near their beloved house on the bluff where they moved after losing their first home in the Vanport flood of 1948. A viewing will be held at St. Agnes Cathedral at 7:00 PM on Friday the 18th of November. A Military service will be held at Willamette National Cemetery on Saturday at 1:00 PM the 19th of April 2010." The family suggests remembrances be made to the Marine Corps' Toys for Tots program.

Arnie, had not exactly lied to me, but he never told me that "he" had been one of the three wounded in his squad. I didn't know the exact story of the Silver Star, but I'm positive it was one of the heroic tales he attributed to one of his men.

I skipped the viewing. I wanted to remember Arnie sitting in his usual chair drinking his customary two pints of PBR, nodding his head and tapping his toes to the blues. As a Marine Corps Vietnam veteran I wanted to thank Arnie for his service to our country. I would be grave side to honor the life of Staff Sergeant Arnold Mills.

A black limousine climbed the long driveway of Willamette National Cemetery. It pulled up next to a small pavilion where there was a casket draped with the American flag. I was on the perimeter of the area watching the scene unfold. Two people got out. I didn't know the young man. Maybe it was a grandson, but the other person was Velma holding a bouquet of red roses. The rows upon rows of white crosses always seemed to be lined up no matter which way one looked at them. They climbed and descended gentle slopes like a giant rolling wave of white crosses. She laid the roses on a grave, but whose? What more had I missed during our many talks?

The family and elderly were seated in front of the casket. The rest of us huddled in a small group at the edge of the structure. I was the only one from the tavern. A lieutenant colonel barked "Atte-e-en-hut!" A bugler sounded "Taps." Two corporals in Marine dress blues began crisply, yet solemnly folding an American flag. After a few words, a good-looking Marine with a chest full of medals showing his tours in Iraq handed Velma the flag. He took off his white glove and gently shook her hand as she said "Thank you." His eyes, had seen combat and no longer had that youthful gleam, but they were filled with gratitude as he offered his condolences and "Appreciation from a grateful country and the United States Marine Corps."

The Marines were assembled and smartly marched off the grounds. The small crowd had left. I was alone as I walked down to the row of crosses where Velma had placed the roses. There were remnants from many visits.

The inscription: "Patrick Mills, Pvt. USMC—March 12, 1948—August 5th 1968 KIA Republic of South Vietnam." They had not only lost their house to flooding in '48, but they lost a twenty year old son in Vietnam.

Arnie could have told me lots of sad stories, but our conversations were always upbeat, looking towards the future, and how Velma's memory seemed to be getting a little better. Maybe he was right. She remembered where to place the flowers.

Driving back to Vancouver, I wasn't sad. It was a good ending to a life well lived, but I had the blues. The kind that have only one cure. When I entered the house I grabbed my wife by the hand and said "Come on dear, we're going over to the Mock Crest. It's about time you heard the Eagle Ridin' Pappas play da blues." She was too stunned to say no.

We ordered, what else, a Blues Burger Basket. We were now the senior members in the tavern sitting at the small table with an empty chair. Like Arnie and Velma, we became invisible to the young folks. I vowed to break the mold of our generation.

A young man walked past obviously looking for a place to sit. Recalling the first time I met Arnie, I pointed to the chair and said, "Have a seat young fella." His eyes quickly scanned the room for a better opportunity, seeing none, he said "Thank you" and rested his well tattooed muscles on the arms of the captain's chair. My wife squirmed in her chair at the sight of his tattoos. We had always thought that only low-life's and drug users sported tattoos.

Determined to change the stereotype attached to seniors I said "Tell me about your tattoos. I've always wondered how a person picks a tattoo that they will have for the rest of their natural life. And would you like a PBR?"

"No thanks" He said. "I don't drink anymore. In fact, see this flying eagle? The date on the banner in its talons is January 1, 1998. That's the day I gave up alcohol and drugs. I like to tell people 'I've been soaring like an eagle ever since.'"

In that instant, I was immediately freed from my many biases about the tattooed people who sat in "their" corner of the bar. It was liberating. Like us, they were there for the music. I said "How you doin' tonight," to a tattooed, purpled haired girl I had always ignored. She said "I'm doing great and is this your wife?" The barriers were shattered!

The band tuned up with a cacophony of sounds and mic checks, I ordered a PBR for myself and two diet cokes, one for Ardi and one for our new friend, Brent. The blues never sounded so happy and the PBR never tasted so good. I raised my pint and silently said, "This one's for you Arnie Mills, Semper Fi!"

***

Riff Raff
(Reader Choice Award Winner circa 2013)

by Bob Ferguson

I would attack them from a hiding place in plain sight. They would never expect an assault from a pariah of society. I planned to steal enough of their money to skip to Portugal or South America and live comfortably for life. Except—I had no life. They took it when they hooked Jess, my son on drugs—and he overdosed.

Drugs are every parent's nightmare. At our wits end, we used the tough-love technique espoused by the current psycho-gurus and kicked Jess out of the house the day he turned eighteen. Through teary eyes at his funeral my wife, Jenny said "We drove him straight into their ripping claws." She was right. The guilt, self-hate was intolerable. Ten days after his service Jenny found the easy way out—sleeping pills.

There was no celebration of life, no service, and no obituary for either of them. They were each buried with a simple marker in the family plot where I had expected to be the first to rest. After the burial I numbly headed home. No purpose. No feeling. No reason to live. On the two-lane road back down the hill it would be easy to give the wheel a quick jerk to the left into the path of an on-coming semi-truck. Swift. Quick. Sure. But with every passing second, like an infectious fever, hate began permeating the cells of my numb body. As a driving force, hate seemed more dominant than love. Vile loathing was giving me an insidious purpose for living—to seek retribution. They would pay dearly for what they had taken from me.

Parks had always been a pleasant place to while away a few hours with our family. Birds liked the high canopies of the tall oaks and centuries of adaptation had superbly equipped the squirrels for climbing trees more nimbly than Olga Korbut on the balance beam. I had no one to enjoy it with. I was wretchedly alone. The sounds and sights held no joy.

The park was further degraded, by the scum of humanity scattered about in old quilts, filthy sleeping bags and the rags on their backs like a human garbage dump. They reminded me of the dregs of the second wine bottle I was devouring. As disgusting as these human vermin were, they would be good camouflage for me to carry out my vengeance in the place where I knew Jess first began using drugs—the Park Blocks.

My .38 snub nosed service revolver that I had carried in Vietnam gave me a feeling of protection. It was stuffed into the field jacket that I had picked up at a surplus store. My gray hair was matted and matched my five days of stubble. The black stocking cap made me indistinguishable from the other homeless people who were in various stages of reverie induced by booze or drugs. I had become Charles Bronson in "Death Wish." Life was imitating art.

It always surprised me that buying drugs was so easy. I wondered why a prosecutor simply didn't grant amnesty to the guy at the lowest level if he ratted on his supplier. Then that supplier gets amnesty if he finks on his source, right on up to the top. I would prove my own theory. I would wait for the mule, the delivery man, the creep that made it possible to get my son hooked. It would be easy to follow him to his connection and follow that link to the next guy in the chain of command. I couldn't offer amnesty, but a .38 in his face would be even a more convincing argument to become a stoolie. After I killed a few, they would know that Portland is no place for pushers.

"I'm Joe," I said to a guy on a park bench as I screwed off the top of a fresh bottle of vintage MD 20/20 and handed it to him.

The Colossal Life of Mr. Average

"My wife was Jenny, my son was Jess. We called ourselves the "J" family," I continued trying to be friendly.

"They call me Riff, I used to play the guitar on stage," he said before he took a deep swig like it was the elixir of youth and he wanted to be a teenager again.

"I'd like to score a little Mary Jane," I said trying to sound like an entrenched user.

"Haven't heard that term in a while. If you mean pot, just watch that corner down there and you'll see a guy who seems to talk to everybody. I'm tapped out or I'd give you some."

It was a generous offer from a guy who seemed to be on his last legs.

"Keep that bottle of *Mad Dog*, I appreciate your info," I said sauntering off toward a bench that had just become available with a better view of the corner.

His pants hung so low I wondered what held them up. A black baseball cap with a flat bill was stuffed sideways on a thick head of black hair. He was, it pained me to admit it, a handsome Latino. Even under his baggy hoodie you could tell he had a powerful build. Long silver chains draped down his sides and seemed to have no purpose other than decoration. He had mastered the art of smoking while at the same time, talking incessantly on a cell phone.

It was a week day and he was busy. It was a quick reach into his fanny pack, a simple handshake, hug or short huddle and that was it. Money, pot, and short greetings were exchanged. It surprised me how many people dressed in suits and ties shook his hand. A bank of gray clouds created a sun screen (one of the prompts) that added an even darker mood to the nefarious activities taking place right in front of me.

He periodically got into a white, pimped-up Honda with dark tinted windows. He would be gone for a little while and then reappear on the same corner after stepping off the light rail stop just across the street.

The day was getting away from me. The Charles Bronson in me wanted action, but if I was careless it would be dangerous, maybe fatal. I feigned sleeping, reading the newspaper and if a stranger walked by, I would even ask for spare change just to blend in with the vagrants.

The mark I had selected for my wrath would not be easy. He appeared to work alone, but there were always a few guys that looked just like him standing nearby. "His homies in hoodies," I chortled to myself. It had been a long time since I had chortled, but it was not the good kind. I decided those stupid chains must be some sort of Ninja weapon. Even if they weren't, he might be carrying and getting him alone would take some doing. They were wary, always looking for cops, rival gangs, and whatever other threats druggies face. They looked at me, but only saw the lowest of all life forms sitting on the park bench. Hiding in plain sight was perfect.

After a few hours the white Honda came by and he again got in. I glanced at my watch. It was a quarter to one. In almost exactly a half hour he again hopped off the Max line at the same stop—alone. That was it! I had my first victim in my sights. They had a time schedule for dropping off money and reloading with drugs and it matched the Max train schedule!

In the, invariably out of toilet paper, seedy, and filthy, public restroom, I shaved and washed my face. From my backpack I took out a non-descript jacket. I was ready.

"Riff, I'll give you five bucks to watch this bundle for me. I'll give you another ten when I return, is that a deal?" I asked laying the pack next to him.

"You sure you can trust me?" He said.

"Your cap says you're a Vietnam vet or is that just brag?" I asked.

"No way! I joined the Marines right out of high school," he said looking me in the eyes seeking a clue for some sense of trust.

"Well, Semper Fi my friend. Once a Marine always a Marine and this ol' Marine needs your help, if I'm not back by 5:30 this evening, you can have it all," I said walking away. I knew I had him with the Semper Fi.

Like clockwork, the white Honda came by at 3:45 on their two hour schedule. That meant that my Latino friend would conduct his business with those behind the darkened windshield and according to the Max schedule at his exit stop he would arrive back at almost exactly 4:15 pm., but I had a surprise for him.

I hustled down two blocks where the schedule read the next pickup headed north would be at 4:10 pm. It was in the "Fare-less Square" so all I had to do was hop on and take a seat. The train was deserted. He was easy to spot, sitting in the back of the second car with his feet stretched out taking up an entire seat. I took the seat directly across the aisle from him.

"There's a whole car man, why you got to be right here in my face?" He said in broken English pronouncing "you" like the first syllable of Ju Ju Bean.

"I thought I knew you from somewhere," I said.

"Now dat you know you don't know me, I say you should move," he said bobbing his head in a smart-alec way. I still wondered why the word "you" was such a tongue twister.

Physically, at 60 years old, I was no match for him, but I wanted to slap his silly face. I stood up like I was going to change seats and in a flash I pulled the .38 from my jacket pointed it at his face and said "Don't move! My little friend here says I know you from the corner by the park, now put your feet down and your hands on the back of the seat in front of you."

He stopped smiling. I slid into the seat behind him with the pistol pushed into the middle of his back. I wanted to pull the trigger and just leave him sitting there hunched over, but I had a problem. The gun was loaded with ammunition that was over forty years old and the bullets were green tracers. It was meant to be used as a survival pistol in case the F-4, in which I flew as a navigator on photo reconnaissance missions, was ever shot down. The green tracers were used instead of flares to notify the rescue choppers that I was a friendly force. A snub nose is not as accurate as a longer barrel, but there was a chance it could go clean through a body and ricochet hurting a bystander. I had never fired the pistol. Not even in Vietnam and I wasn't sure what it would do.

"You, you are a dead man," he said in anger making the "Y" sound even more like a "J."

"So are you, if you don't do exactly as I say," I bluffed, cocking the gun and pushing it harder into his back. "With your left hand, unbuckle that fanny pack and hand it back to me. It's got a hair trigger," I lied.

I took the fanny pack while moving the gun to the back of his head.

"Your buddies will be looking for you as we pass the park and what you need to do to stay alive is to wave at them as we go by."

As we passed the park he was waving and I was holding up the fanny pack and flipping them the bird. Cute, but it was immensely stupid on my part. He knocked the gun from my hand, grabbed it and pulled the trigger—thank God the ammo was manufactured by the lowest bidder. It didn't fire. I had a second chance and pulled a lock-back knife with a 5" blade from my pants pocket. He was unimpressed. He pulled out a 15" bayonet.

The train jerked to a stop, the doors opened and a passenger jumped on and quickly clubbed my enemy from behind with a policeman's night stick.

"Semper Fi," said Riff. "I saw his amigos scattering when they thought they'd catch hell for losing the money and the pot. Then I saw him knock the gun out of your hand so I ran to the next stop. Lucky for you I always carry this souvenir night-stick for protection. A cop lost it in a park scrum a while back."

The dealer was stirring as we hopped off. We ran back to the park, grabbed our gear, and hailed a cab. It felt great to strike a blow for the good guys.

We gave the money to a homeless shelter, and the dealer resembled a body that was fished out of the Willamette River a few days later. The police speculated he had stolen some money and drugs from a local gang. Go figure.

Riff needed a place to live. I needed company. He'll be living with me for a while. He's a pretty good guitarist. He plays and sings on open mic nights at a few blues joints. We've gotten involved in some veteran's causes and my problems seem no worse than many others who are putting their lives back together.

I suppose life can imitate art, but it's better to leave the vigilante stuff to the trained professionals. And what became of the pot? We're Marines, not saints for cryin' out loud.

***

Occupy The Bacon

by

Bob Ferguson

    The tragedy of lightening is that it strikes randomly. It never smites the deserving. Have you ever heard of lightening striking an "idiot or congressman?" As Mark Twain, said "...but I repeat myself." That was the view held by Angus Thornberry, a cop who walked the "Old Town" beat until a quirky accident, changed his life.

    While walking his night shift, a bicyclist riding a "fixie," the type of bike with no gears, no brakes, and no brains, slammed into him. The rider's thick helmet crashed into his cranium giving Angus a concussion. Like many other cops, Angus filed for the "golden disability parachute." His reputation suffered when he claimed to have Post Traumatic Stress Disorder shortly after taking acting classes.

    Angus' brain damage was minor, but career wise, it was catastrophic. The injury left Angus with an intolerance for the "bacon maple bars" at Voo Doo Donuts. He could no longer order their world famous, "bacon maple bars" without becoming nauseous. While standing in the long line to order this epicurean delight he had been keeping an eye on the back room meetings of a subversive group labeled the FBMBS, Free Bacon Maple Bar Society. Their dastardly plot was to coerce Voo Doo Donuts into accepting food stamps for their awesome maple bar concoctions.

    While Angus' attorney, Sue Early deliberated with the union about his disability, he was determined to work until his claim was settled. He transferred to another precinct and became a

The Colossal Life of Mr. Average

police clerk. At the heart of the claim was how much money he deserved for a donut disorder and his nebulous, PTSD.

The next year, Sue won Angus $6 million from the helmet company of the fixie rider for its dangerous design. He would also receive tax free disability payments of $120,000 per year from the Public Employees Retirements System. Angus now enjoyed being a one percent fat cat. He had been through 3 years at the Portland Police Bureau and at 29 years of age he felt entitled to an opulent retirement. He would protect his personal property values, by ridding Portland of its panhandlers and any distasteful denizens that crossed his path. They would move on or be roughed up by his goons while the police turned a blind eye. He had placed an imaginary noose around his acclaimed part of the city and would tighten the knot until the last of the unsavory characters moved on.

The FBMBS movement gathered steam. During the good weather, large groups would occupy city parks with their signs, dogs, and disdain for the wealthy. On rainy days, smaller groups huddled in the heated bus shelters. Like most well-meaning protestors, they were docile until they got stirred up by "extremists." Angus would direct his ire at these vitriol spewing agitators.

Angus began with a campaign against "bikes with no brakes." It passed by a wide margin. Oregon is a Nanny state. At the Saturday market a vendor named Ruby sold clever <u>song birds made from vinyl records</u> (one of the more creative prompts that I remember.) He branded her as illiterate for using the revered platters of Elvis Presley. He wasn't totally heartless. He actually liked the twisting of the Beasty Boys into something that looked like the Maltese Falcon. But the insult to Elvis was too much. He used his perverse influence to bar her from the market.

Angus thought he was the biggest man in town. He lived in the top penthouse of the tallest condo building in Portland. It had a 360 degree view. He owned many of the buildings that cast their flickering lights onto the night landscape. When he looked at Mt. Hood he could only think of his many business interests along the way to the slopes. He hosted frequent galas on his expansive, top of the building veranda. He was the top dog.

His first year on the job, Angus Thornberry had been a good cop. He often helped many homeless get what they needed on a cold night. But when he began forcing them to Vancouver, they all agreed it wasn't the concussion that changed him, it was the money. Greed had consumed Angus. He filled his coffers by legal, but unethical means. He alienated everyone he had ever known. His selfish ruthlessness knew no bounds. He was a real life Scrooge found in Dickens' *A Christmas Carol*.

While standing on his palatial rooftop looking at a <u>Blue Moon</u> (prompt) Angus was struck by lightning that burst forth from a single cloud. A YouTube recording captured the thunder clap that sounded ominously like a voice saying "You really beaked me off!" The video anomaly has been compared to seeing Jesus in a potato chip. Others believe it was an answer to prayers.

Only the funeral director attended the service. He held a strange sympathy card in his hand. He read it to an empty room. "Thank you for creating such publicity about my vinyl Elvis song birds. I can't keep them in stock at the Pearl Works Art Gallery. I rephrased these words from my Mark Twain collection, "I'm sorry I didn't attend your funeral, but I approve of it." Ruby.

Thorsday Nights

by Bob Ferguson

The young man next to me was whizzing like a race horse while I was peeing in Morse Code—symptomatic of an aging prostate.

"It must be hell to get old, eh ol' geezer" snorted the young stallion in the stall next to me. His tone insinuated that senior citizens should stay home at night.

"Well, you'll never find out if you don't show a little more respect," I said.

"Oh you must be one of them Vietnam vet, tough guys huh," he said emerging while zipping his fly.

"Could be," I said while pulling at the paper towel dispenser which was usually empty, but miraculously had three sheets left—I took them all, "But I didn't get old by getting drunk and being stupid," I continued.

There is a restroom etiquette that is observed by all men—don't let your eyes wander and keep your mouth shut. He had transgressed good behavior in the *head* of one of my favorite haunts for live music, The Blue Monk. My wife, Ardi and I are regulars and he was an interloper. Blues man, Curtis Salgado was the headliner and we had arrived early for dinner and good seats. I like to drink more toddies than are good for me; Ardi likes Diet Pepsi and is the designated driver. We are harmless—most of the time. But once in a while when I get to feeling like I'm twenty five, then I can be dangerous. The music, bourbon, and testosterone coursed through my veins that night and made me feel youthfully bullet-proof.

"You callin' me stupid old timer?" He said in a voice reminiscent of a young gun-fighter trying to spur John Wayne into a showdown.

Re-checking my fly, I left without saying another word. The intruder was in his mid-thirties, wore a Boston Red Sox hat backwards on a sloped forehead giving him a definite Cro-Magnon look. His black T-shirt was emblazoned with a University of Oregon big yellow "O." However, his remaining ensemble of old jeans and worn sneakers clearly labeled him as a pseudo-alum or wannabe fan. He did not fit into the tony crowd of the Belmont Street neighborhood. He was a thug with hairy knuckles.

No other venue in the Rose City offers such good blues, great food and minimal cover charge than the "Monk." The time slot of 7:00 PM to 9:00 PM was perfect for a Thursday night out and that's what made us regulars. The trespasser kept giving me the evil eye the rest of the night making it uncomfortable for us.

We climbed out of the Greenwich Village style basement of the Blue Monk and Mr. Cro-Magnon followed us. Out on the street I pulled up my collar as Thor sounded his thunderous alarm for an approaching summer gully-washer.

"Hey ol' geezer, did you know you looked like a frog in a blender when you were dancing?"

Technically…he was correct. When I get to shuckin' and jivin' I kind of lose myself in the music. But *my* dancing wasn't the point. This was an impudent challenge and the hackles on the back of my neck bristled. Was I old? Yes. Could I ignore such an insult? Never!!

To Ardi's horror, I turned and faced my antagonist. "Did you know that wearing that hat backwards at your age makes you look like an immature, stupid twit?"

"Well why don't you do something about it you ol' geezer," he said with a zeal fueled by alcohol. Then he gave me a rather vigorous shove like a bully on the playground.

It would soon be fisticuffs and I was no match for him. But, when the forecast called for thunder showers and Ardi had just had her hair done, that put a collapsible umbrella with a solid wooden handle in my grip. As lightning flashed, brilliance struck. I swung it like Thor's hammer, (a prompt) Biblically smiting the bully with the heavy stock squarely upon his schnozzle. While he writhed in pain we ran and laughed the quarter of a block to our car and stormed out of there as fast as any Prius could possibly storm.

That night I learned three things. First, an umbrella has more than one use. Second, my dancing style hasn't changed in fifty years. Third, when all is said and done, there really is a Thor.

Chapter 6

At This Age, Let 'er Rip!

***

My attempts to make a million dollar killing by importing an entire ship load of fertilizer from Venezuela in 1973 ended up as good intentions. I had seen the fertilizer shortage looming for months. Per usual, I was a few weeks short of acting, recalling one of my favorite phrases, "A day late and a dollar short."

When the Exxon Valdez spilled its load of oil in Alaska I had the temerity to call the vice president of Exxon and offer a solution. Dr. Rick Parker, a friend from our church was a brilliant biochemist and had patented a process to clean up oil spills. The technology called Bio-Remediation uses oil eating bacteria to literally eat away the oil. Unfortunately, the public outcry for polluting the pristine environment of Prince Rupert Sound demanded an immediate public relations solution. So Exxon went with the ultra-expensive, far less effective clean up method of wiping the beach with rags and putting the rags into landfills to be monitored…forever.

Rick complimented me on a nice try, but nice tries don't make the millions. It was a heart-pounding, exciting prospect for a week, but it consumed every waking moment. This gave birth to the *Fergism* "Failure will not deter me, but it sure tires me out!"

Along the way I've had some moderate successes. There was the Richardson Shin-guard, mentioned earlier. We more than doubled our shin-guard investment in that first year. The year the Portland Trailblazers won their NBA Championship, Jack Ramsey used a plastic beaded jump rope to condition his players. I knew the local manufacturer from my sporting goods days and negotiated for the retail rights, signed up Ramsey for a small licensing fee, and made a bunch of money in only three weeks by selling to everybody's favorite store, Fred Meyer's. They were a ninety store chain.

The next year the Chicago Bulls won the championship. On a small budget I went to Chicago, stayed at the YMCA, and rode the bus to various sporting goods dealers. Nobody bought the rope even though I paid the NBA for the rights to use the Bulls logo.

Undaunted, I called on Sears at the very tip-top of the Sears Tower. It was embarrassing. I had to take a number and wait just like the DMV. After a very long wait, my number was called.

"Salesman 39, what is your product?"

When the other salesman were all called, they went down a hallway to a conference room. I didn't know what to do. I leaned over the receptionists desk to talk into the intercom speaker. "I have a plastic beaded jump rope used by NBA teams."

"Salesman 39, are you still there?"

The receptionist pointed up to a speaker in the ceiling. As calmly as one can do, I looked up at the speaker and repeated my spiel. There were snickers around the room from sales veterans.

"I have a plastic beaded..." I said, before being interrupted.

"Do you have a million dollars in liability insurance?"

"Well, uh, er, no, but if you buy from me I will get it." I said.

"We don't do it that way. Please come back when you are prepared," said the pleasant, matter-of-fact, voice from on high.

Avoiding eye-contact with the chortlers, I packed up my goods, tucked my tail between my legs, and walked out into the worst Chicago winter on record. Even the severe weather wasn't as biting as my Sears reception, but I can't complain business was always good. When one door closed, another door would open.

***

Getting Off The Couch at Sixty One

My boat was adrift on the fickle sea of life and I only had one oar in the water. My childhood dreams of becoming rich and famous had floundered. My airy hopes for huge success became flotsam mingling with empty beer cans and assorted bottles swirling slowly atop an oil slicked eddy in the backwaters of a fair-to-middling life. Life was good, but not great.

The mound of sand in the bottom of my "Life's Hour Glass" was a non-descript dune of plain-vanilla color and growing at an alarming rate. The remaining pile in the top of the glass seemed smaller as time raced by. Reality set in. It was clear; there would be no cure for death in my lifetime.

The excitement of the business was gone. I had been *schlepping* sporting goods and advertising products around the northwest for thirty years. The sales managers I worked for were now younger than my kids. I began to let Rachel do a lot of the business. The daily energy tank was emptying sooner and the *power naps* seemed to creep up on me more frequently. The sands would soon be gone and I was still hitting life's snooze alarm.

Absolute panic set in. Then one day the theme from "Rocky" blasted me off the couch. The words invaded my brain. The song reverberated through my body stronger than a bazillion decibels of sound pulsating out of gigantic speakers like those at a Stone's concert. I was stunned. No radio or CD player was on. The song rekindled the fire in my belly. I realized that at 60 years of age I could still do something significant in life. I was compelled to act. It was like an epiphany from God, I jumped up and said "I'm going to be a teacher!"

Fantasticness would have to visit me in my next life, but I would make sure that the rest of the sand falling through that tiny hole brightened the entire pile of monochromatic grains on the bottom of my hour glass.

Teaching meant lifelong learning with a greater purpose than merely scratching a sales pad. Being around kids always made me feel young. When I now awakened from a power-nap I felt old, not refreshed. It was a no-brainer. I still had VA educational benefits that would help offset the cost of getting a Master's In Teaching degree. With Rachel working in the business, a new research tool called the internet, and taking only education classes I could knock it out in a year at City University and keep the business thriving. This was a Colossal opportunity!

The classes were held in a small business complex not too far from our home. It would require lots of work, but I could do it The first day, in the largest room of the complex, we were asked to stand up and tell the class a little bit about ourselves. The majority of the forty students were in their mid-twenties, a few in their early thirties, and most had jobs to pay for their school. As I faced the group, the advice of my kids came back to me, "Dad, whatever you do, don't act like a know-it-all and just blend in." I had used that *modes operandi* my entire life. I decided to be bold and hope for the best.

The self-introductions told of undergraduate work. One of the students said he "speaks five languages," another already had an MBA, but wanted to teach, and yet another had a BA in education, but was getting her MIT degree to upgrade her credentials. The competition would be stiff. After all of the short, but energetic speeches it was my turn.

"I feel like Strom Thurman must have felt every time he addressed the US Senate. He would see an audience of colleagues who were at least thirty years younger than himself. Hopefully, that's where the comparison stops because he was in his nineties. My main credential is that I've done a lot of things right to live this long. I'm Bob Ferguson and I look forward to this adventure."

The Thurman line got a lot of laughs. They seemed to like my elder sense of humor. I recycled my old jokes and the comic relief in classes seemed appreciated. I could get away with things the other couldn't so I pushed the envelope and found there was still a lot of excitement in life.

Going back to school was a re-discovery. My grades were excellent, I learned more about the computer than I ever wanted to know, and the kids were delightful to be around. Learning about the Mayas, Incas, and other ancient civilizations has been enriching. While in Mexico on a cruise ship I visited a Mayan village. I would have loved to have had that experience before teaching that section. It was fun to be an educated tourist, as opposed to the "Ugly American."

Teaching a segment on memoir writing to a group of seventh graders is still paying dividends even as I write this part of my life's script.

Class has been dismissed for over a decade, but my audacity for being irreverent continues to grow. The beauty of being old is that my cheekiness is oft-times mistaken for senility and my sarcasm is seen as being old-school. A few debates have started when I ask people to stand for the Colors as they pass by or take off their hat for the National Anthem – I really don't care what they think and you can "Take that to the bank!"

Chapter 7

I'm In

At any party they find each other and drift off into the kitchen to speak in a strange language. They talk delightfully about "crushing blows," "big hits," and the "deep threat." They are a fraternity without a secret handshake. I listen, but know I can't join in. I am not one of them. I didn't take the vow to work for five cents an hour. They are football coaches.

Paul Durham, our Linfield football coach and athletic director was fond of saying "Linfield produced more P. E. teachers than Oregon and Oregon State combined." The majority of them became coaches. That, in fact, was his recruiting strategy which he dubbed "The Tentacle Method." Send a lot of coaches out into the world and they will send players back to you." It worked and the longest streak of winning seasons began. It is sixty years and counting. It is the longest streak in any sport at any level! The guys in the kitchen would talk about the kids they sent to Linfield. I admired them. In three hours of practice they would have more teachable moments than teachers would get all day. I often lamented that I had not chosen coaching as a profession even though I put in thirty years at the "Pee Wee" level of nearly every sport. Enjoyable, fulfilling, and all that, but not a profession.

"So you wanna be a coach? You always said if a job ever came up to let you know. Well, I'm lettin' ya know." That voice on my cell phone was a longtime friend who had just retired from forty years of coaching football—from a wheelchair.

In college we called him AC, an acronym for Alley Cat. He had a habit of sneaking down the alley to the back door of our favorite watering hole, The Blue Moon. The passing of fifty years does not warrant the change of a nickname. They are for life.

"What have you got going on AC?" I asked.

"The guy they hired at Days Creek decided not to coach and they asked me to take his place for just one year. It could be a lot of fun," he said.

Often I had carelessly said, "I'd like to be a coach." It was now time to see if I would adhere to my own favorite sayings "Walk the Talk," "Put up or Shut up," and "Fish or Cut Bait."

"When does the season start?" I asked, more out of curiosity rather than thinking of penciling it into my calendar.

"We check out gear this Friday after school at three. Since today is only Wednesday we can handle the gear if you can't make it that soon. Then we have a little camp next week just to see what we've got," he said.

Being a paid football Coach was a "Bucket List" dream, but at age 65 and not yet retired, my response might take several days of pondering. There were other people to consider. I would have to finagle a transfer of my business obligations to Rachel, commute 228 miles one way, twice a week, and come home only on weekends for four months. This obligation would give anyone pause for thought. I knew Ardi would understand…wouldn't she?

After a nanosecond I said, "Okay, I'll be at your house by two and we can go up to the school to hand out the gear after class."

That previous March, I had again attended the University of Oregon Football Coaches Clinic. It was followed by the Forman

Football Camp in June. It had become my annual "Must Do" event. Earlier I had written about the camp in an article for the Roseburg *News Review*. A copy of that article follows. You'll need a magnifying glass. That's the nature of self-publishing.

Sunday, June 18, 2006—The News-Review   **SPORTS**   Roseburg, Oregon, Page D3

Small town camp enjoys top-notch coaching

EDITOR'S NOTE: *Bob Ferguson, 63, is a 1965 graduate of Linfield College. He has spent most of his working life as a manufacturer's agent, until he received a masters in education two years ago. The following column was inspired by a book he hopes to have published in a year about ordinary people doing extraordinary things. He can be reached at 360-254-1224 or email, robefergus@aol.com.*

Bob Ferguson
Commentary

CANYONVILLE — This small community hosted an extraordinary event — the Days Creek Football Camp — two weeks ago.

The camp combined superior football knowledge with the evangelistic passions of coaches eager to spread the gospel of football to kids from the fifth grade through high school. The volunteer coaching staff included former NFL and college stars as well as a national high school football coach of the year.

A trio of University of Oregon football line coaches headed by Steve Greatwood began the day by teaching young linemen the basics of the three-point stance. They quickly moved into action drills, the pass rush and pass protection, while thrashing tackling dummies in the process. These coaches attacked the drill, even with the young kids, with the same intensity they would bring to a group of their college veterans who were expected to lead the Ducks to the Rose Bowl.

The quarterbacks were getting professional-level tips from the head coach at South Eugene High School, who happens to be NFL Pro Bowl quarterback Chris Miller. You can't do better than learning from the best of the best.

Defensive backs were immersed in their position through the masterful coaching style of Todd Shirley. He is a Linfield College product and is cut out of the same coaching cloth as the great Ad Rutschman, the former long-time grid coach at that school. Currently, Shirley is the head coach at Powers High School.

The Ducks' running back coach, Gary Campbell, put his charges through the same drills he runs his Pac-10 players through. The NFL veteran was clearly having as much fun as the sharp-looking fifth grade athletes who were all eyes, ears and grins.

John Wolf, the camp director, is an assistant coach at Days Creek. As a former Duck player he is the UO connection for the camp on schedule with an infectious enthusiasm.

Gene Forman, head coach at Days Creek High School, is the catalyst for the camp. He does an extraordinary job of recruiting coaches like Shirley, who played for Forman in high school. Being a Linfield alum, he helped guide his protege to that school. The two men now compete in the same league, but the affection they share for one another transcends league boundaries. The UO coaches sign on because they realize Forman, "Is doing this for the kids."

Preston O'Hara, another of Forman's former players, brought his sons.

"I knew they would get great coaching from coach Forman. I played for him, and I wanted my sons to learn his brand of football," O'Hara said.

A mother of two campers chimed in, "This is a miraculous thing for such professional coaches to come to tiny Canyonville for our kids. It is by far the best experience my boys have ever had in football and they can't wait until next year."

Besides the outstanding quality of the coaches, this camp is special because of the brief talks given by those men. They emphasized goal setting, academics, respect for parents and teachers, perseverance, and work ethic.

"Be the best that you can be," was a common theme throughout their talks. The closing comments for the camp were reserved for Marshfield head coach Kent Wigle, the National High School Football Coach of the Year.

As he put his hand on Forman's shoulder he said, "One of the best things about football is that it builds great friendships, like I've had for many years with my dear friend."

Football was the subject matter, but good character was the curriculum for the day. As the mother of the two sons said, "Those kids who went skateboarding, or stayed home to play video games really missed the boat."

107

It's fair to say that I have had my share of "Late-Life Crises." A few include using my VA educational benefits to get a Masters in Teaching degree at age sixty one, getting my first paid coaching gig at sixty five, writing a book, and becoming a fan of live music round out my zaniness. Ardi was surprised, but not shocked when I told her about the coaching gig. Her response was "I think you're out of your mind, but you'd hate me if I didn't go along with it." The stage was set. Another exploit was eminent.

The trip to Roseburg was as long as I had remembered, and there were still thirty miles to go! The directions to Shoestring Lane in Riddle, Oregon took me to the home of the Alley Cat, Gene Forman. His abode would be my "home, away from home" for four months. It was modified with ramps to accommodate the wheelchair of the man for whom a Linfield College Hall of Fame award has been named. Recipients are people who have succeeded in life while "overcoming extreme adversity." Worthy adventures require dedication. Coaching demands your soul.

The ten mile highway from Riddle to Days Creek School passes by the Seven Feathers Casino. The road is filled with blind corners, and pickup drivers irritated with city-dwellers gawking at the Colossal scenery. The hills collide together in an overlapping tapestry of late summer grass the color of a bay horse. The jutting, red-bark trunks of Madrone trees starkly contrast to their high crowns of broad green leaves. Gigantic Douglas Firs and outcroppings of nearly black, granite rock complete the landscape of Van Gogh splendor. When the angled rays of late fall strike the oaks and maples, the forest looks afire. For four months this trip regaled me.

My job was to be the assistant Junior High Coach of an eight-man football team for Richard Therial. However, the death of his father, back in New York made it impossible for him to fully participate. So, I was thrust into the job of "acting head coach." The X's and O's of football had moved on since my playing days, but the blocking, tackling, and running fundamentals were the same. That's why they are called "fundamentals." We would run the same plays as the varsity so it would not be "rocket surgery."

It was my full intent to squeeze as much out of the experience as possible. I wrote a blog on the school web site that chronicled our games. If the kids spotted a misspelled word I would do 3 push-ups for each error. Every week, to the delight of the kids, I did 9 push-ups. Hey, at 65 I was lucky to do that many! The remainder of my coaching story is not a golden reflection on the venture, but is closer to verbatim vignettes written nearly a decade ago. These are a few blogs and scribblings from that experience.

8-26-08

The junior high coach is still in New York tending to the details of his father's death. I take the kids for this practice. It's a blast! Taking a few pages out of John Wolfe's and Jim Bob's book we have some lively drills. (Two coaching friends of AC's who helped conduct our pre-season mini-camp.) The kids look good. Being head coach for a day is fun. I give my twist on what I've learned so far. I'm not a hard-liner, but I am firm and they respond with enthusiasm—that makes me enthusiastic, which makes them more enthusiastic. I like being the head coach of a handful of kids.

The 15 kids range in size from 4'8" and 66 lbs. to 5'10" and 160 pounds. A player over 140 lbs. cannot be a running back. That makes good sense. I think we look pretty good and I will be coaching them in a jamboree next Thursday-September 4th. (After the game I have to drive to Bellevue, WA. to keep the business going – about an 8 hr. drive.)

8/27

Shangri-La it ain't! In this bucolic setting one would only expect top notch kids. "Taint so!" Three of the best athletes have to apply for hardship cases to attend school. They have drug/home problems and we discovered yesterday that one player had a little something extra in the energy drink that he was swigging down during the water breaks. He became goofier as practice wore on and he crapped out completely on the second sprint during the conditioning part of practice.

Coach Forman got a call early the next morning from the Athletic Director who informed him that three parents had called him about the player's language and drunkenness.

The problem every coach faces is, do you cut the kid and lose him to the dark-side or do you try to work with him and get him back on track. I liked AC's approach.

"I'm growing a garden here. It's a beautiful garden of gladiolas." I don't think of him as old, but I'm certain the kids think the massive, gray haired man in the wheelchair is ancient. "It can be a glorious garden, but I've got some weeds in my garden. It's up to the gladiolas to take care of the weeds and you all know what I'm talking about."

The offending player couldn't get his act together and went to live with his grandmother in California. He was our best player and would have been an All-Star in the league. In eight-man football you only need a few great players to win a state championship. He was the best hope for the varsity and we lose two more stand-outs as well. Every coach has to play the hand he is dealt.

The pleasant wave between the drivers of passing cars in the small towns is a custom I have promoted ever since I left Riddle. At first I thought you had to know the other driver. Not so. It's a friendly greeting that no doubt reduces road rage.

Another routine I liked was the conversations that took place while waiting in a line at the bank, grocery story or post office. While picking up AC's mail at the post office a small man walks in with a basket of fresh vegetables. His gray hat had been chewed to tatters and has some short strings hanging from the bill. I can't resist.

"What kind of dog you got," I ask.

"Pit bull," he says flashing a grin missing several teeth. "She's just a pup so she loves to chew. Got my shoe too," he laughs as he points to his tennis shoe wrapped in duct tape.

Another man walks in and immediately asks "What happened to your hat?"

The five people in the small office broke out in laughter as the story was repeated and the shoe, again, became the center of attention. Our friend with the chewed hat and shoe gave his basket of vegetables to an appreciative clerk. He chortled as he said "See you all later," as he merrily dashed out the door. This was much more fun than the all-serious, can't you hurry-up, attitudes found at my local post office.

We began the season with fifteen players. We won our first game. The second game looked like it was men playing against boys. We lose three kids for the season and another becomes ineligible. We are down to eleven players. They have to play wherever they are needed. We are using our fourth quarterback. Coach Therial is still in New York. My main job becomes Head Cheerleader. We lost one game 46-0 and I was depressed, but Rick Neuheisel should have been in a coma—UCLA lost 62-0! And Rick got paid a ton of money!

After a particularly bruising loss I asked our kids "What did we do well?" "We tackled hard," said one. "We had good pursuit," said another. "We played until the whistle blew," chimed in a small voice. They weren't as orchestrated as an opera, but to my ears, each of these small, boned tired, proclamations was an aria by Pavarotti.

October 20, 2008

Every coach takes their job home with them, but this may be ridiculous. At 3:00 AM, Ardi wakes me up and says "Stop pushing me in the back and telling me to get in there on the kickoff team."

"What team did I put you on?" I asked sleepily.

"The punt team, now go back to sleep coach," she says.

Relieved we're not a man short on the kickoff team I go back to sleep and dream of recovering the on-side kick.

So far, being a football coach has literally been a *Dream Job*.

November 23, 2008

John Madden once said "I've never worked a day in my life. First I was a player, then a coach, and now a TV football guy." Could it be true that coaches don't work? The answer is, "Of course they work!" Every profession has a down-side. Madden didn't like the cross-country bus rides, movie stars don't like endless rehearsals, and high school coaches don't like doing the team laundry or disciplining kids for breaking team rules. But using the Gestalt concept that the "whole is greater than the sum of its parts," it's true, coaching isn't a job, it's a joy. As definitive proof, in addition to my many coaching friends, I offer millions of coaches in every sport who have had coaching as their life's passion.

To be an authorized, officially anointed coach I had to sit through a lengthy class on a sunny Sunday in Salem to get "credentialed." The class was really about "Do *this* or you might get sued." It also covered "Do *that* or you might get sued." It was akin to one of Madden's bus rides from Tampa to Seattle – long, but there would be fun at the end.

What I found odd about the class was that it never emphasized the three goals I felt most important during my thirty years of coaching soccer, baseball, junior high wrestling, basketball, volleyball, and tee ball. Maybe they were too obvious:

1. Do your Best. (A lot of times things were topsy-turvy, but I gave it my best shot and I expected the same from the kids.)

2. Have Fun. (If it's not fun for you, it won't be fun for the kids.)

3. Love the Kids. (The first two are easy, but kids are not all born with the same amount of lovability.)

It's my theory of coaching that these simple goals are what keeps coaches coming back year after year. After all, it sure beats working for a living.

AC's wife, Jackie was on a several month trip so it was only the two of us. We laughed every day, talked football incessantly, and drank a lot of blackberry wine made in the garage of his friend, Jim Bob. It was a lot like living in the old Theta Chi fraternity house at Linfield College, but we had a little cash to spend.

During the days, I continued writing *Some Days Chicken, Some Days Feathers*, my new "Flip-Phone," the discovery of a Wi-Fi hot spot at a restaurant kept me in touch with business matters, and every single day I couldn't wait to meet the kids in the locker room.

Ardi and I still attended the Linfield games on Saturdays. At one of the tail-gate parties one of our friends heard the story that I was coaching with AC. He remarked that the 228 mile drive was a "Heckuva commitment." Others echoed similar thoughts.

It's a matter of perspective. Our season was half over and never once had I thought of my coaching gig as a *commitment*. During the four hour trip I used the books on tape to listen to the classic, *The Invisible Man* by Ralph Waldo Ellison. (His parents had a lot of chutzpah to name their black child Ralph Waldo. He had no choice. He was destined to be a writing genius.) His book is as relevant today as it was when it won the National Book Award back in 1953. The hours flew by.

The sea battles of Horatio Hornblower, by C. S. Forester steeled me to face a band of youngsters waiting to explode upon the world with pent up energy accumulated by sitting in required classes. For two hours I would be privileged to be a small part of their world. It was an *opportunity*. I never gave one whit of thought that it was a *commitment*.

Our record was 1 win and 5 losses, but I count this last journal entry as proof of a successful season.

November 8, 2008

"Thanks coach Fergy," said one. "Thanks for coaching us," said another. We then gathered as a team one final time and did Popcorn. The players jam up together, jump up and down like kernels in a popper and yell something that they make up that goes with our theme for the game like "No quit in us" and it always ends with "Go Pups! It was our last game. We got pummeled. But to an observer watching the endorphin producing spectacle our kids were performing they might have thought we had just won the league championship. Win, lose or draw, we always went into the locker room on a high note.

As I watched them play that game, the thought that this was my first and also my final football coaching gig weighed on my shoulders like a two ton tackling dummy. I knew the last day would come. Every date of great joy or miserable sorrow penciled in on life's calendar inevitably arrives and delivers its message. It can't be avoided. We can only enjoy the good days to the fullest and weave and bob so life's round-house, hay-makers become merely glancing blows.

During their later years some extraordinary people travel to the ends of the earth to do incredible things, like missionary work or building schools. I admire their tenacity, but I found a Colossal adventure in an easy, four hour drive from my home to greet a bunch of junior-high kids waiting to do Popcorn.

***

Chopped Liver

Jack's shock of gray hair, movie star good looks (albeit an aging movie star,) gregarious, over-the-top friendly, personality, make him a "Babe Magnet." On Monday nights, we are regaled with Gypsy Jazz by a band whose name sounds like Chinese take-out, the "Kung Pao Chickens." The band, swing dancers, and Jack are the entertainment.

A few years earlier, I had stumbled into the *Laurelthirst Public House* and ingratiated myself into his kinship. He offered me a seat at his habitual, front table. Over the years, from our vantage point, we have met a menagerie of characters, had bushels of laughter, and I always receive a massive injection of delight.

The mix of the "Chickens'" music, Pabst Blue Ribbon, and the laughs at our table were so addicting that I became more religious about making it to "The Thirst" on Monday nights than a Rabbi going to Shabbat.

One evening, as the band wafted a medley of Django Reinhardt tunes into the warm night air, a curious event occurred. During the band's break, a young lady sidled over and sat on Jack's lap. The well-proportioned lass wore a black, scooped neck, top that was deficient in holding her ampleness. Her jeans were as tight as yoga pants. Ruby red lips matched her cranberry shoes. She resembled a working girl, and I don't mean a secretary. Jack didn't blush. He's not the type.

It was a draw between who was more shocked, Jack or her boyfriend. Who quickly said "Why are you suckin' up to a couple of guys who need Viagra?"

"I can assure you, this guy doesn't need Viagra," she retorted.

We had noticed, but ignored them in the adjacent booth, except, for an occasional glance at her over-scooped, sweater.

"You are the most handsome, debonair, and sophisticated person in this place," she said while running her fingers through his hair. "I love the way you dress, so casual yet classy."

Jack does wear clothes good, but classy? His wardrobe is tastefully purchased off the high end rack at the Salvation Army. I'm thinking something a bit more honest would be *"a purposely rumpled ensemble that was undeniably 'fashionable' …for its previous owners."* But, at "The Thirst," Jack is one of the better dressed denizens. His taste in clothes adds to his genuineness.

While ignoring me without so much as a "howdy," she slathers Jack with more platitudes.

"You look so smart," she says draining the dregs of an expensive drink.

Swirling the ice in her empty cocktail glass she places it in front of Jack. The non-verbal message is "Lookie there big boy, it's empty. How's about buying me another drink." This wasn't Jack's first rodeo, but even he's taken aback by the peculiarity of his new found lap fixture. Especially since her portly boyfriend, with a very forgettable face had joined us at our table.

By gently cooing, "I'll bet you're a very, very successful business man." she makes the blatant suggestion that, *you're so loaded, why not buy me another drink*?

Allowing myself to be totally ignored is not my style. I have to get in the act. With arms wide open, in feigned outrage, I blurt out "So what am I, chopped liver?"

We came close to snorting PBR. The laughter breaks the awkwardness. We relish the translucent attempt of an apprentice hustler trying to hoodwink a journeyman rascal.

The band returned and tuned up. Because she provided us with an enormous amount of giggles, Jack bought the poor girl a drink. Her boyfriend drained his cocktail and puts it on the table in front of me. "You haven't told me how wonderful I am so you can buy your own drink," I said.

As the band played on, the two interlopers slunk back to their booth. Jack and I continued chuckling while enjoying the unique sounds of the "Chickens." When the pair skulked out the back door I'm sure they thought of us as a couple of foolish old geezers, which is true. But on that night at "The Thirst," Jack and I were not the "Oddest Couple."

Chapter 8

Bar Stool Chats of Staggering Genius

While writing "Some Days Chicken, Some Days Feathers" I discovered live music almost exactly as written in the story, "My Summer of Blues" on pages 77- 85. The Mock Crest became one of my favorite bars. The music was addicting. The guitars stirred my soul. Live music became as important as food, but far less fattening.

The beauty of a "joint" filled with a diverse group of patrons is that they are all united by the music. You have something immediately in common. Conversations begin. Never having been shy and always interested in people, I can't help myself so I always strike up conversations in most establishments. My invasion of their privacy has been rewarded many times over. My notebook is filled with 3 x 5 cards that capture many of their thoughts. In no particular order of reverence, they appear below.

* "I Told my wife 'I'm sorry I forgot your birthday, but you've had so many lately.'" And he lived to tell about it!

* "The perfect baby-sitter is...Nyquil," said a young mother named Sharon Fluids.

* "I'm a whisky farmer trying to grow champagne."

* At the Blue Moon in McMinnville I met Ivan Rodriguez, a day-job worker. He had become a US citizen. "It took me two years to get here, but I did it" he said. "Why did you come to this country?" I asked. Without hesitation he said with unabashed pride, "Because it's the greatest country in the world!" When it comes to immigration, we could use a few more like Ivan. It was a privilege to buy this patriot a libation.

* A Vietnam vet was buying a few of my books for some friends. "How would you like me to inscribe these books?" I asked. "Legibly" he replied.

* "The evening is measured by how much I've been pleasured."

* "Don't make me get up the Chicago in me!"

* "When it's my time, I want an IV with a steady drip of the 60's music and Olympia beer."

* "...and that, my friend, is how life is and now my tale is told. So enjoy each day and live it up before you're too Dad-gummed old." After this fine attempt at poetry my new, well-oiled, friend says "Okay, you try to think with only 2 brain cells."

* "What's your name?" I asked. "Young Woo," he says. The set up was just too good to pass up. "Young Woo! Well I'm Old Bob," I blurt. The surrounding patrons laugh with us.

* "Is that a tattoo? Oh, I'm sorry, it's a liver spot."

At the Landmark Saloon, where I like to listen to country music at the 6:00-8:00 PM gig I walk in one evening and it's crowded with a bunch of new faces. A guy sitting across the table from me has a great tan, bulging biceps, well-trimmed goatee, and some sort of odd-looking, ugly, Mohawk haircut with a badly receding, old-guy hairline. Dapper in every way except for his new hair-doo.

I have to say something daring to this mostly, well-groomed man. At times like this I have found that 99.9% of the time it works out. I say to Mr. Tan Biceps "Did you fall asleep in the barber's chair?" He smiles and says "No, I always get an ugly haircut whenever I can." We both crack-up and become instant friends. I always like my odds in taking a chance. I encourage you to give it a try. It embarrasses my wife, but I am shameless.

* "This place is 50 shades of gray…hair."

* "Want to hear my joke?" I ask. "Oh, I'm just a pile of excitement," replies the bartender.

* "That's funny enough to make a chicken grin."

* A band member was being teased by an audience member and he responds "Hey, do I come down to the car-wash and heckle you!"

* Overheard at "The Thirst" (Laurel Thirst Public House) "I wish I had met you 30 years ago. You'd have been 10 and I'd still be in jail."

* "I wish I had matured as fast as I've aged."

* A band member makes his pitch. "Our CD is a million seller. We've got a million of 'em in the cellar."

* "I got divorced and immediately lost 300 pounds."

* At a Karaoke bar some friends commented on a performer's lack of singing skills. He replied, "I'm not here to sing, I just want to be heard."

* "Got real drunk once and told the hotel guy the hot tub isn't hot and there's not much water in it. Then he says, 'that's because you're in the wading pool.'" (Given the story teller-possibly true!)

* "Love is in the air...or somebody is just cleaning the grill."

* At Linfield football games we have promulgated some tailgate doozies. One nagging wife was trying to get her husband to leave the merriment in the middle of a good party. A rascal says "Don't be a wife, be a buddy." Per usual, the wife won.

* "The number one rule of dancing is that the woman never makes a mistake – my mother told me that."

* A band leader talking about rude patrons; "We don't tell them to go to hell anymore. We suggest they find a warmer climate."

* As I was sipping a pint, I say to the guy on the barstool next to me, "This PBR costs the same as the Wall Street Journal I bought this morning." "Ya," he says, "but the PBR doesn't make you any smarter."

* "What's the difference between the National Guard and the Boy Scouts?" Everybody is stumped. The Marine says "Nothing."

* "What on earth are you doing leaving half a glass of PBR! Don't you know there are millions of children in China who would love to have that!"

* "Give your best to my wife...I think I said that wrong."

* Matt makes Tincture. He says it has a "subtle" effect. Dr. John a regular at The Thirst for the Kung Pao Chickens says "There are a lot of 'subtle' people at The Thirst."

* The latest DVD for the "Kung Pao Chickens" makes the music sound as good as any I have ever heard. John Neufeld, the guitarist that made it in his home-studio said "I am obsessed with

passing on the music in the best possible form." A group of us gather at the front table every Monday night to listen to this band. The price is right, it's Free! We call ourselves "Chicken Heads," ala Jimmy Buffett's "Parrott Heads." We know we are listening to Django Reinhardt's music in the best possible form.

* "My only health problem is age."

* At the former "Lucky's" bar I was sitting outside at the smoking table with some patrons. I'm a newcomer and mention that I had just drifted down from the Laurelthirst only a few blocks up the street. A young fella pipes up, "First time I've been here too. Every bar I go into has to have a 'healthy dose of suspicion.'" The cast of characters certainly provided that edge. Lucky's was a biker hang-out, mixed with customers who wore their best "Goth" clothing, and what really brought out many a ne'er-do-well were the cheap drinks.

Willie was a Lucky's regular. He was a short, thin, friendly, black man who loved soul music. The bar-keep frequently gave him some money to select the Juke-Box music. I got hooked on Willie when he sang along with the music and it sounded like Lou Rawls singing a duet with himself! When he mentioned that he followed Linfield football, a free drink was always delivered to his customary bar-stool. Willie became an instant friend.

Lucky's was torn down a few years ago and Willie has passed on. Occasionally I stumble into a bar that serves cheap drinks and has a good juke box on the mere "suspicion" that Willie's doppelganger will be crooning to a Lou Rawls tune. He was such a beloved character in the neighborhood that the following picture has been placed in the upper-left corner of the Memory Wall at the Laurelthirst Public house.

R. I. P. Willie

    * This is a true story from Lucky's Bar: "Is that your purse?" a rough looking biker snidely asked. He was referring to my black, writer's satchel my kids had given me for my birthday. "No, it's where I keep my .38, it's not as convenient as my shoulder holster, but it's less conspicuous," was my canned response to foil hecklers. It always did.
    "You don't say," he comfortably drawls. He eyes me and continues. "I keep my .45 in my saddle-bag right here."
    I had been one-upped and called out! "Okay, it is my purse, it's where I keep my lipstick, in case you want me to kiss your butt." Laughter broke out around the campfire located in the back yard of Lucky's.
    I have since attached my Vietnam dog tags to the strap. Now nobody calls it my purse. A few times I've been asked if the dog

tags are real. I say "Yes, I wear them for the kids who didn't come home." That response has brought a few tears to some inquirers. I love toting my satchel and replying to the remarks it often brings.

It has meaning. My kids gave me the satchel. I've sold more copies of my book, "Some Days Chicken, Some Days Feathers" out of my "purse," in bars than any other marketing scheme. A conversation starts, the mention of my Vietnam book comes up and I take it out of the satchel. They sometimes blink when they learn that my pricing structure is $20 dollars for an "Unsigned" copy, $10 dollars for a "Signed" copy, and $5 dollars if you are a Vietnam vet. Marine Corps, Vietnam vets usually get a free copy.

* On a summer "Harley Night" at the Cascade Bar and Grill a biker tells me of his adventures and says "I've ridden through all of the lower 49 states. How many states have we got anyway?" I say "54." He declares, "Well, you can only ride through 52 of them." The tragedy is that he votes!

* "Any allergies?" The doctor asks Jack Forde, a divorced friend of mine who is telling the story at a Linfield tailgater. "I tell him yes," says Jack. "What are they?" Questions the doctor. "Wedding Cake." I'm sure the doctor laughed as hard we did.

Once in a Blue Moon I am caught without 3x5 cards. Those with double ** indicate they were written on a napkin, coaster, bar menu or first available piece of scratch paper.

** "I like what George Burns said 'I'm going to live forever. So far so good.'"

** "Dang it! I'm not dating her. I mean, I'm not dating her, dang it!"

**At a VFW club I'm talking to a vet who has a slightly clubbed foot. He wanted to be a soldier and go to Vietnam. "How in the world did you get in?" I asked. "When they told me to put my foot on the little step, I put up the same foot twice," he chortled. "How did it work out for you?" I asked. He gave a great reply, "No problems, just challenges."

** "I've been married seven times. I've had more wives than I've had the common cold."

** "Did you ever call one of your wives by the wrong name?" I asked. "Nope, I used 'Honey' for all of them."

** "That's a true rumor!"

** "I'm either in trouble or I'm working my way out."

** "A DUI is a sobering experience."

** "How are you?" I asked an old-timer. He replied, "Is that a trick question?"

** "I've been married 44 years. Boy, that sounds like a sentence." A witty imbiber responds, "It is a sentence, there's a subject and a verb."

** "I quit drinking for a girl named Brandy."

** "Thanks for your Republican dance. For *Mustang Sally*, you were very conservative."

** "It's a short story. It only seems long."

** "I had to break up with her after she left me."

** "I may mix my metaphors, but I never mix my drinks."

** "What are you buying your wife for Christmas?" I asked. "A pen so she can pay the bills."

** Comparing recent trips to Austin, the traveler said "The Texas Caviar tasted a lot like bean dip."

** Hoping for a little romance a wife says to her husband, "Look at how that husband is looking into his wife's eyes." The husband, a few sheets to the wind says "He's an optometrist."

** The Blues is an aria with beer.

** "That's an example of macular degeneration right before your very eyes."

** While talking about short term memory a patron said, "The only thing I retain is water."

** "I fell in with evil companions…and had the time of my life!"

** "Don't die until you're dead."

** "If you think life is boring, wait until you're dead!"

** On a break with a band member we started thinking of a few old sayings and came up with these gems:

- My elevator may not go all the way to the top, but I've managed to stop at the important floors.
- I may not be the brightest bulb in the pack, but I cast a bright light for my friends.
- I may not be the sharpest tool in the shed, but I've hammered out a lot of good things in my life.
- I may be a little light in my boots, but I've had to stand tall many times in my life.
- I may be a few bricks shy of a load, but I've carried more important weight than bricks.

Chapter 9

Pickleball Addiction

The best unofficial therapy for joint replacement, stroke, cancer, heart attacks, and most serious maladies is not covered by Medicare, Medicaid or Kaiser. Despite the lack of insurance support, it seriously improves one's mental and physical health. It's not a potion, pill, exotic diet or lotion. **Warning**! This therapy is **addicting**! You will find yourself in a new circle of friends who carry paddles, sweat a lot, and often offer up unsavory wails, grunts and an occasional Dad-gummit (or similar facsimile) of lament. The common name for this miracle therapy is Pickleball! The scientific term is…Pickleball (what did you expect?) It has nothing to do with pickle juice, pickled beets or pickles. It is a fast paced, rapidly growing, all ages, sports game with a vegan name.

My Pickleball friends were asked to describe in only six words, this fastest growing sport in America (I found this on the internet so it must be true.) A few of their responses follow:

Pickleball Rescues
Old, Exhausted,
Tennis Players

By Ernst

Pickleball is
Addictive, Frustrating
Vigorous, Social

By Linda

Playing Pickleball
Is My
Lifeline

By Curtis
(Only 5 words, but close enough for government work.)

The game is played on a volleyball sized court; 44' X 20 feet. The height of the net is easy to remember, it's one "Yardstick" or 36" high. Two PB courts fit onto a tennis court so it is a popular outdoor game. As someone once asked, "What's the difference between tennis and Pickleball courts?" The answer, "The Pickleball courts get used."

The only tricky rule involves the "Kitchen." The Kitchen is the line exactly 7' from the net. You cannot hit the ball while standing "In the Kitchen" unless it has first bounced. But that's enough about rules. (I've never read a rule book that excited me.)

There is an official rule book and instruction videos on line. The rules are similar to tennis. The game is played with a plastic ball with holes in it and paddles larger than a ping-pong paddle, but smaller than a racquetball racquet. One Pickleballer describes the game as "Ping Pong on steroids."

The most expensive racquet and a year's supply of balls will not cost as much as your shoes! All good stuff, but the joy of Pickleball is in the friendships created that extend beyond the courts. It's good people having great fun.

Do your mind, body, and soul a favor, get involved in Pickleball ASAP. Age, joint replacements, and heart attacks are no barrier. I played in a tournament where two participants were in their 90's. They won no medal, but received the only standing ovation of the day. I am entered in an upcoming tournament billed as "Dinosaur Doubles." The ages of the players are combined to determine their bracket. My partner is Dee, a survivor of multiple cancers. We are one of the most senior duos playing in the 151 years and over group (AKA the Jurassic Period?) We fully expect to be semi-competitive with the other Dinosaurs in this Colossal event. We do not think of ourselves as dinosaurs. We think we are Dino-mite! Game On!!

Chapter 10

Meanderings, Musings, and Mutterings,

***

Meandering

The house sits at the end of Blue Heron Lane. It is the legacy that John and Myrtle Erikson left to our family. Though she was ever the pragmatist, nurse Myrtle was so affected by the ideal setting that she wrote poems about their "Little cottage by the sea." They need their own book. In their later years, they sold the house in town and lived permanently at the beach. The unique, irreplaceable setting makes it the crown jewel of our chattels. It is now our responsibility to pass it on to the next generation.

Samish Island is best seen from a bicycle. The views of Padilla Bay are panoramic. The homes vary from the "Little Rock Cottage" to the vaulted ceiling, rustic cedar sided, mega house. Both enjoy sweeping seascapes. Nestled among the magazine-worthy abodes sits a quaint, turn of the century, small farm house with a detached garage-shop-shed. The sign in the front yard is more weather-beaten than rustic. In sky blue, script lettering against a white background it proclaims "Smith Boat Shop."

Fred lives in the house that was once his mother's. Brother Don lives elsewhere on the island. The large, well maintained lawn, and rose beds predict that if they are as particular about boat building as they are about home maintenance, they make a stellar product.

For thirty years in their wood-stove warmed, garage-shop-shed they have built a small sailboat classified as a "Pelican." It is a twelve foot, gaff-rigged, squared fore and aft, boat that resembles a small Chinese Junk. With three foot sides and covered bow it is a sea-worthy craft originally designed by a Naval architect. The designer built it for his kids to sail in the San Francisco Bay so it is extremely safe. The boats are so ugly they are cute.

The brothers built up a following, founded the Pelican Fleet, and guided camping trips to, where else, Pelican Island every fourth of July. Their business model was "Good ol' boys in coveralls, building a superbly crafted boat for a price a family could afford." We bought one. My friend, Art Smith liked it so much, he built one. For several years I sailed in a few of the fleet races, camped on various islands, and enjoyed immensely our multi-colored sail boat we dubbed "Rainbow."

Fred and Don Smith built boats in their multi-purpose building for thirty years. They decided to retire, held a big retirement party in their shop, announced to everyone in the boat trade that they were going out of business, and alerted the Pelican Fleet that someone else would have to take over the camping trips and racing regattas. It was a neat and tidy departure.

The Monday after the retirement party Don <u>meandered</u> up to the shop only to find Fred sitting on a sawhorse drinking a beer from a small, but well stocked fridge.

"What do you want to do now that you're retired?" Asked Don.

"Well, I've been sittin' here thinking. I think I'd like to build boats and go camping in the islands. What about you?" Fred asks.

"Can't really imagine anything else I'd rather do," said Don.

"We just got an order in today, should I call them and tell them we're back in business?"

"It's a good thing we didn't sell any of our tools," said Don as he began selecting lumber for another Pelican.

It must have been a wonderful realization to discover that while it was called "work," they couldn't have enjoyed it any more even if they were "retired." They worked/retired several more years until Don's passing. A small plaque and tree at the Samish Island Community Center remember the life of Don. We should all be so lucky to have jobs that we want to continue in retirement.

Musings

- I've often <u>mused</u> that life is not black and white or even shades of gray. It's bursting with eye-popping colors, exploding with mouthwatering tastes, and soul soothing textures of opportunity that are for our taking.

- Celebrate before you're "Celebrated." Be Brave, Bold, and race to end.

- Old stories are like listening to a "Golden Oldie" that you haven't heard for a long time. The music is lovely to the ear, but a story is beautiful to the heart.

- In my business, my philosophy was "If I can't get the job done in 8 hours, I work 9. If I can't get it done in 9 hours I work 10 and so on. There's only one way to get the work done, that's to do the work." Pretty simple. Very effective.

Mutterings

Lately I've been <u>muttering</u> to myself about the state of our politics. The tsunami of arrogance in The Donald and Hillary campaigns makes one talk to one's self. Someone observed and it seems self-evident that "Poli-Tics is a group of blood-sucking bugs." Having had a foray into politics as a candidate for State Representative in the seventies it was clear this definition is being kind. Politics is a tornado of self-interest. It was a great education, but a profession that demands no conscience.

If I were "King For A Day," here are the edicts I would enact:

To vote you must first:

Observe a first grade class for three weeks, teach the class for a week, and then decide if teachers are paid enough.

Figure out how to make the monthly payroll of a small business even though the business made no profit that month.

Serve the homeless at a Rescue Mission during the months of January and February.

Take the bus/bike/walk to work. Any mode, but a car.

Live in only half your house for two months.

Spend a few days in jail as an inmate. No special privileges.

Stand on the corner filthy, haggard, and scruffy with a sign that reads "Anything helps, God Bless."

Volunteer on a political campaign, coach a team, ride in a Humvee in Iraq, or write a letter to the editor. Pick two.

You must <u>earn</u> your right to vote through community service.

This pontificating author has either done these things or has enough first-hand knowledge to empathize with the circumstance. None of these edicts promises you "Free Stuff!" It's too bad we don't have a Bill of Responsibilities next to our Bill of Rights.

***

Your Story, Your Book

Dabbling in the written word has convinced me that our history needs to be recorded as we lived it. Without our witness, our stories are rearranged or completely disappear. Aided by the ease of publishing, getting others to write their tales has become a mission/passion. So in the spring of 2016 I hosted a series of memoir workshops at the Hillsboro Senior Community Center.

"Your Story, Your Book" is a workshop that was conducted from 10:00 AM to noon on four consecutive Fridays in April of 2016 and repeated in 2017. The first hour was spent teaching the craft of memoir. The second session was spent demonstrating the simple computer instructions needed to put their story into book form. The Center had Wi-Fi so by using my laptop and a large monitor it was easy to physically show the minimal skills needed for self-publishing.

By the end of the workshop, three of the five participants had published their books! The other two were on the verge of submitting their final drafts. It would be my hope, now that I have this curriculum, to take it on the road and get others to publish their stories. If you wish to be informed about workshops, email me at robefergus@aol.com.

The only socially redeeming quality of this epistle is to encourage everyone to write their own story. *Some Days Chicken,*

Some Days Feathers has taken me to Frederick, Oklahoma to eulogize Jerry Bennett, the only Vietnam casualty from that small town. Someone heard about the book and I was given this amazing offer I couldn't refuse. Several surviving relatives from his family of twelve children and some childhood friends attended the ceremony held in the town square. It was a privilege to be a part of this "Norman Rockwell Moment."

The cover picture on this book was taken on the stage of the Austin Playhouse. Due to the *Chicken* book, I was part of a marvelous, three week production of "The Telling Project." It is five or six vets weaving their stories into a theatrical production. Write your story, you never know where it will take you!

The End

Not Even Close!! Future projects: Stories of the Vietnamese Boat People, Workshops that will put YOUR Story into YOUR Book, and more shenanigans.

(For comments, inquiries, and where to send large amounts of cash, please email me at robefergus@aol.com)

ABOUT THE AUTHOR

Like many of you, I have survived a few age related health issues and adjusted my gait to fit the new joints. Life now revolves around the grandkids, Pickleball, live music, and writing endeavors.

Many people like to travel, but I enjoy the journey of seeing old friends, meeting new people, keeping Portland Weird, and learning new things that keep my gray cells, gray. Until the sun sets for the last time, I am going to do all that I can to embellish my journey. Thanks for being part of this Colossal trek by reading this tome.

Made in the USA
Coppell, TX
14 January 2022